PagePlus X5 User Guide

How to Contact Us

Our main office
(UK, Europe):

The Software Centre
PO Box 2000, Nottingham,
NG11 7GW, UK

Main:

(0115) 914 2000

Registration (UK only):

(0800) 376 1989

Sales (UK only):

(0800) 376 7070

Customer Service/
Technical Support:

http://www.support.serif.com/

General Fax:

(0115) 914 2020

North American office
(USA, Canada):

Serif Inc, The Software Center,
17 Hampshire Drive, Suites 1 & 2,
Hudson, NH 03051, USA

Main:

(603) 889-8650

Registration:

(800) 794-6876

Sales:

(800) 55-SERIF or 557-3743

Customer Service/
Technical Support:

http://www.support.serif.com/

General Fax:

(603) 889-1127

Online

Visit us on the web at:

http://www.serif.com/

International

Please contact your local distributor/dealer. For further details, please contact us
at one of our phone numbers above.

Credits

This User Guide, and the software described in it, is furnished under an end user License Agreement, which is included with the product. The agreement specifies the permitted and prohibited uses.

Trademarks

Serif is a registered trademark of Serif (Europe) Ltd.

PagePlus is a registered trademark of Serif (Europe) Ltd.

All Serif product names are trademarks of Serif (Europe) Ltd.

Microsoft, Windows, and the Windows logo are registered trademarks of Microsoft Corporation. All other trademarks acknowledged.

Windows Vista and the Windows Vista Start button are trademarks or registered trademarks of Microsoft Corporation in the United States and/or other countries.

Copyrights

Contents

5. Working with Text.. 99

6. Pictures, Lines, and Shapes..........................173

7. Colour, Fills, and Transparency.....................223

1 Welcome

Welcome!

Welcome to **PagePlus X5**, the award-winning Desktop Publishing (DTP) solution from Serif. PagePlus is the easiest way to get superior publishing results, whether on your desktop or via professional printing. It's simple for anyone to create, publish and share their designs as outstanding printed documents, stunning PDFs, PDF slideshows, stylish websites and eye-catching emails.

To make life so much easier, PagePlus comes with an impressive selection of design templates, creative gallery content, and styles for you to use. As a result, publishing to a professional standard is easily achievable for experienced and inexperienced users alike! You'll also be able to reuse existing content by importing PDF documents and word processing documents. On the flipside, you'll be able to export drawn objects to all the latest graphic file formats.

PagePlus X5 doesn't stop at superior publishing. Its range of design studios makes PagePlus stand out from the crowd—**Image Cutout Studio** for cutting pictures out from their backgrounds, **LogoStudio** for custom logo design, and **PhotoLab** for powerful image adjustment and effect combinations. You simply cannot afford to miss them!

For a more detailed summary of what PagePlus can offer, see **Key features** (p. 4).

Upgrading?

If you've upgraded from a previous version, this new edition of PagePlus includes a host of **exciting** new features (p. 11) which keeps PagePlus ahead of its competitors and at a fraction of the price! We hope you also enjoy the additional power and performance edge.

Registration

Don't forget to register your new copy, using the **Registration Wizard**, on the **Help** menu. That way, we can keep you informed of new developments and future upgrades!

Key features

Before you get started with PagePlus, we recommend you take the opportunity
to familiarize yourself with PagePlus key features and capabilities.

Layout

- **Versatile Setup with Auto-Imposition**
  Just click to specify layouts for small (business cards and labels),
  folded (booklets and greetings cards), and large publications (banners
  and posters)!

- **Ready-to-use Design Templates**
  Fancy a quick route to produce stunning designs for home or business
  use? Adopt one of an impressive collection of eye-catching **design
  templates**.

- **Theme layout design templates**
  Choose a **theme** on which to base your publication! Each theme offers
  a choice of publication types (**Brochure**, **Business Card**, **Flyer**,
  Newsletter, or **Poster**) and differently designed layout options for the
  theme. Pick **multiple layouts** as your new pages, then simply fill
  picture placeholders with your own pictures.

- **Master Pages**
  Save time and maintain consistency by using multiple master pages
  assigned to your publication pages.

- **Layers**
  Each page can have multiple layers—so you can assign elements to
  different layers for modular design.

- **Professional layout tools**
  Movable rulers, guide lines and a dot grid, as layout aids, help you
  position objects precisely; snapping jumps an object to guide or grid.
  Use Sticky guides, a great way of moving (in bulk) all objects snapped
  to your guide lines—move the guide and objects will follow! Align
  and resize to objects using Dynamic guide snapping.

- **Page control**
  Add and remove pages in just a few clicks of your mouse in the Pages
  tab. Drag and drop pages within the tab to reorder sequence. Assign
  master pages to several document pages at once.

- **Mail & Photo Merge**
  With Mail and Photo Merge, read data from just about any source: tables from HTML web pages, database files, even live ODBC servers! Print to labels and letters equally.

- **Tables and Calendars**
  Choose from a range of preset formats or design your own table. Use the convenient Table context toolbar to sort data, format cells, and choose from a wide range of functions for **spreadsheet calculations**. **Calendars** are table-based for enhanced functionality, and support Year update, inline personal events, and public holidays! Even create your own savable table and calendar AutoFormats.

- **BookPlus**
  Treat separate PagePlus publication files as chapters and use the **BookPlus** utility to link them into a book! Assign text styles and colour palettes across publications, automatically generate an Index or Table of Contents, add page numbering and output your final long document to both print and PDF.

Pictures

- **Import Pictures**
  Import commonly-used standard file formats, including RAW digital camera formats. **AutoFlow** pictures (or drag and drop) from the always-at-hand Media Bar into sequential **picture frames**! Import Adobe® Photoshop® files directly into your PagePlus publications.

- **Image Adjustments**
  Apply **adjustments** (Brightness, Contrast, fix red eye, and more) or use **Edit in PhotoPlus**, which accesses Serif's award-winning photo-editing package (if installed).

- **PhotoLab for non-destructive adjustment and effect filters**
  The powerful **PhotoLab** studio packs a punch with an impressive selection of editable adjustments, creative, and artistic effects (pencil, water colour, oil, and more). Use integrated **Straighten**, **Crop**, **Red-eye**, and **Spot-repair** tools for easy **retouching**. Apply filters to selected areas of your photo by using **brush-based masking**. **Save** adjustment/effect combinations as favourites for future use.

- **Quick-and-easy Image Cutouts**
  Image Cutout Studio makes light work of cutting out your placed pictures, directly in PagePlus. Use brushes to discard uniform backgrounds (sky, walls, etc.) or keep subjects of interest (people, objects, etc.).

- **A versatile Metafile Format**
  Import and Export Serif Metafiles (.SMF), a proprietary image format with improvements to the Windows Metafile format (WMF). Better line, fill, and text definitions make them ideal for sharing graphics between Serif applications.

Creative

- **Drawing Tools**
  Design stunning vector graphics with Pencil, Pen and Straight **Line tools**, and add line endings like arrowheads, diamonds, and quills. Alternatively, the array of fully-customizable **QuickShapes** let you quickly create outlines for your designs, while **Convert to Curves**, **Crop to Shape**, and curve drawing offer complete flexibility for creating any shape imaginable! **Mesh warp envelopes** add perspective, slant, and bulge to any object. Join object outlines to create more complex outlined objects.

- **Fills**
  Enhance shapes and artistic text with fantastic professional fills. Use the Colour tab to change fill, line, or text colour with one click. Choose preset fills (solid, gradient, or bitmap) from the Swatches tab's palettes—even create stunning bitmap fills from your own images. What's more, every colour used is added to the **Publication Palette** so that you can easily re-use it again and again.

- **Intelligent Colour Schemes**
  Choose from dozens of preset **colour schemes** to change the overall appearance of your publications with a single click. You can customize the scheme colours, create brand new schemes, and apply any scheme to a "from-scratch" publication.

- **Ready-to-use Styles**
  Choose various filter effects, glows, shadows, textures, and materials from the Styles tab. Customize the preset styles or store your own!

- **Transparency**
  Add transparency to your backgrounds, text frames, tables, shapes and text to achieve a truly professional look. As with colour fills, you can apply **solid**, **gradient**, and **bitmap** transparencies—even create bitmap transparencies from your own image collection.

- **Filter Effects**
  Apply eye-catching **Filter Effects** to make your images and text really stand out. Easily add shadows, glows, bevels, blurs, reflections, outlines, feathering, or embossing effects and alter the flexible settings for exactly the right look—your original object remains intact and editable if you change your mind! Use the **Shadow Tool** for on-the-page control of basic or skewed drop shadows.

- **Astounding 3D Lighting and Surface Effects**
  Advanced algorithms **bring flat shapes to life**! Choose one or more effects, then vary surface and multiple coloured light source properties. Start with a pattern or a function, adjust parameters for incredible surface contours, textures, fills, realistic-looking wood, water, skin, marble and much more. Combine 3D transparency and Reflection Maps for realistic glass-like effects on non-reflective/reflective surfaces.

- **Instant 3D**
  Transform your artistic text and shapes into impressive 3D objects directly on the page! Apply multiple coloured **lighting effects** (with directional control), along with custom **bevel** and **lathe** effect profiles to create your very own unique contours.

- **Connector Tools**
  Easily design organizational charts, family trees and other diagrams—connectors will link your boxes, circles, or other shapes together, with links being maintained during any object repositioning.

- **Stunning logos and flashes**
  Use the Gallery tab for a range of pre-designed **ready-to-go logos** and **flashes**—alternatively, create from scratch in LogoStudio or base your design on existing PagePlus objects! Use **flashes** for advertising on your website, on a poster, or a greetings card.

- **Photo-based borders**
  Exciting new ready-to-go borders can be applied around text frames, tables and pictures alike. Create and save custom borders! The Gallery tab's **Picture frames** have the same borders already applied.

Text

- **Import text power!**
  Add word processing content to any text frame—**Word 2007** (and earlier versions), **Open Office**, **Rich Text Format**, PagePlus's **WritePlus**, and many more text formats.

- **Text Frames**
  Compose story text in **text frames** then easily position, rotate or size the frame to suit; connected frames host the same story text and can be filled automatically by **AutoFlow** or manual text fitting. Enhanced **text wrap options** and separate crop and wrap outlines mean you have greater control over where text flows and how it appears. Import, paste, export text in **Unicode** format... design with a foreign-language or special fonts and characters. Text paths also benefit from intelligent text fitting.

- **Anchor any object**
  Anchor **pictures**, **shapes**, **tables**, **artistic text**, and **nested text frames** to your publication's artistic or frame text. Position horizontally and vertically in relation to anchor point, indented text, column, frame, page margin guides, or the whole page. Flow text around floating objects in your text frame.

- **Text Control**
  Apply text formatting from an on-hand text context toolbar; apply **multi-level bullet and numbering schemas** to your paragraphs, even to your text styles; a Text Styles tab for allocating text attributes to chosen paragraphs; flexible bullet, numbering and indenting buttons; and much more!

- **Fonts**
  Substitute missing fonts when opening third-party publications or PDFs. View your currently installed font set in the Fonts tab, including those most recently assigned to text, favourite fonts, and those considered Websafe. Hover over a listed font for an "in-situ" **font preview** of your selected text—simply click to apply the new font if you like it! Easily **swap** all selected instances of a common font for another font in one fell swoop!

- **Frame and Artistic Text**
  Create text with stunning transparency effects, gradient/bitmap (photo) fills, 2D/3D effects and more. Use designer **artistic text** for high impact headlines and powerful design elements—artistic text scales, flips, and can follow a drawn path, while **frame text** flows and line wraps.

- **Find & Replace**
  Search through story text for words and phrases but also text attributes, particular fonts, colours, special characters (Unicode), regular expressions, and words at specific positions in sentences.

- **Text Composition Tools**
  Includes **word count**, **spell-checking**, **thesaurus**, and **proof reader**. **Auto-Correct** and **Underline spelling mistakes as you type** proofing options are at hand.

- **Table of Contents & Index**
  Create automated **Tables of Contents** and **Indexes** for complex documents. PagePlus refers to the named styles you've allocated to headings, subheadings and titles to automatically create your Table of Contents, with up to six levels. Indexing documents is simple too, use the intuitive tools to select important terms and let PagePlus do the rest.

Publishing and Sharing

- **PDF Import & Export**
  Import **individual PDF pages** or **whole PDF documents** as new PagePlus publications. Alternatively, **insert a PDF document's contents** into existing publications. Either way, PDF contents can be easily edited within PagePlus—the text and paragraph formatting of the original PDF document is maintained. Export your documents to PDF, with powerful options to publish your PDFs for professional printing (PDF/X) and the web (streaming supported).

- **PDF Forms**
  Create your own electronic **PDF form**, requesting information from form recipients. Your recipients can type in their responses, then save, print or submit their form electronically. Serif will email you completed forms, or you can set up your own web submission service.

- **PDF Slideshows**
  Create attention-grabbing **PDF slideshows** with stylish page and layer transitions—even add sound and video clips! Share with friends, family, and colleagues.

- **ICC Colour Profiling**
  Set up ICC (International Color Consortium) profiles for your monitor, printer and scanner, and be confident that your printed colours will closely match their appearance on-screen. Avoid wasting time, paper and ink!

- **Printing**
  Print documents professionally on your home printer—as several pages on one sheet, or for large format printing, a single page across multiple sheets. For desktop printers without duplex support, use the **Manual Duplex** printing to create any double-sided publication.

- **Email your publications**
  Share your PagePlus documents natively or as HTML emails, complete with text, images, and active hyperlinks visible in the body of the email.

- **Publish To Web**
  Design your own website directly in PagePlus or publish pages originally created for print to the web as well. PagePlus's intuitive Web Publishing mode creates all the background HTML code for you and guides you seamlessly through publishing your documents and websites online (either in full or incrementally).

Management

- **Managing resources**
  List fonts, resources, and pictures used in your publication in the powerful **Resource Manager**. **Preview**, **relink**, **export**, and **replace** individual pictures and other resources. For fonts you can preview, check if embedded, locate fonts on the page, and export them.

- **Package your project**
  Gather together your project's supporting files to allow your project to be used on a different computer or at a print bureau. Resources such as fonts, linked graphics, linked media files, and more, are embedded in a project **package**—you'll never suffer from missing resources again!

New features

Creative

- **Gradient and Bitmap Fills and Transparency on Outlines** (see p. 234)
  Get even more creative with your object outlines! Apply **linear**,
  elliptical, **conical**, and **bitmap** fills and transparency around shapes
  and text frames for eye-catching design.

- **Colour Scheme Designer** (p. 229)
  Create your own schemes from **colour spreads** based on accepted
  colour theory (**Monochromatic**, **Complementary**, **Triadic**, and
  more). You can add suggested colours automatically, or mix your own
  colours to create the new scheme.

Ease of Use

- **Enhanced Layers** (see p. 47)
  Objects and groups now display under their layers in the new-look
  Layers tab. Great for selecting, reordering, naming, and managing
  text, graphics, and other objects in more complex layered designs.

- **Lasso Selection** (see p. 64)
  The **Lasso Tool** selects specific objects in complicated designs more
  easily. Simply drag around the "target" object to include in selection.
  Use **Alt**-drag with the Pointer tool for the same effect.

- **Hover-based indication of Selection** (see p. 63)
  For use in more complex multi-object page designs, objects "glow" on
  hover over to indicate selectability.

- **Easy Object Rotation** (see p. 77)
  Once selected, objects can now be rotated using a "lollipop" rotation
  handle, preventing accidental rotation.

- **More powerful Master Page control** (see p. 41)
  Assign multiple master pages to your page for even more flexible page
  design. For more design freedom, promote master page objects to your
  page, making them detached and available for independent editing.

Printing and Publishing

- **Interactive Print Preview with print-time imposition** (see p. 247)
  Try out the exciting new **Print Preview**, packed with both preview
  and imposition options—create **books**, **booklets**, **thumbnails**, and
  tiled print output all **without prior page setup**. **Step&Repeat** and **N-
  up** options are also available.

- **Easier than ever Printing!** (see p. 245)
  Try PagePlus's **Print** dialog for the options you need, when you need
  them! With a focus on everyday printing options, including **scaling** of
  your print output, the printing process becomes more intuitive and
  logical.

- **PDF Publishing** (see p. 255)
  Scale your PDF output up or down to a percentage value. Non-
  printable or hidden layers can be included in your artwork when
  publishing to PDF.

Advanced Publishing

- **Cross-references** (see p. 145)
  Insert **cross-references** throughout your publication which reference
  headings, or anchored **text**, **tables**, **pictures**, or **diagrams** which
  update automatically. Insert your cross-reference as a **page number**,
  heading/anchor name, **numbered list number**, and more. Add
  Continued From/To cross-references to text frames.

- **User-defined Variables** (see p. 150)
  Set up your own **variables** to automatically update common terms that
  repeat throughout your publication. Great for updating product names,
  product versions, and language variants all at the same time.

- **Professional-level OpenType Font Features** (see p. 126)
  For advanced typography, PagePlus fully utilizes all your OpenType
  font features—**ligatures**, **stylistic sets/alternates**, **small/petite caps**,
  case-sensitive forms, **fractions**, **ordinals**, and many more are now
  available to both characters and text styles. You can now insert
  characters as glyphs, rather than Unicode characters!

- **Mixed Page Number Formats** (see p. 59)
  Use different number formats (Arabic, Roman, or alphabetic) for your
  publication's front page, intro pages, table of contents, or index.

- **Mixed Page Orientations** (see p. 36)
  Add landscape pages to your portrait-oriented publication, and vice versa. Useful for presenting your wide tables and charts on landscape pages.

- **Improved Colour Management** (see PagePlus Help)
  Manage colour for multiple images with different embedded ICC profiles—allow or ignore image colour conversion to the document's working space. RGB and CMYK images display correctly to screen and print. For PDF printing, choose different **PDF/X1-a output intents** for PDF colour management in professional PDF publishing. Create accurate PDF output of greyscale images to greyscale colour space.

Importing

- **Import Scalable Vector Graphics** (see p. 178)
  Add SVG files (including compressed) to your publication—great for inclusion in your web pages.

- **Import Microsoft Word 2010 documents** (see p. 101)
  Just as for Word 2007 documents you can now import Word 2010 documents directly into text frames!

- **Import Custom User Settings on Upgrade**
  Upgrading from PagePlus X4? Now preserve your **custom Gallery content**, **object styles**, **preferences**, **user dictionaries**, **keyboard shortcuts**, **PDF profiles**, and much more—all from within PagePlus X5.

Installation

System Requirements

Minimum:

- Windows-based PC with DVD drive and mouse

- Microsoft Windows® XP (32 bit), Windows® Vista, or Windows® 7 operating system

- 512MB RAM

- 656MB free hard disk space

- 1024 x 600 monitor resolution (Use of Large Fonts may require a higher resolution)

Additional disk resources and memory are required when editing large and/or complex documents.

Optional:

- Windows-compatible printer

- TWAIN-compatible scanner and/or digital camera

- 3D Accelerated graphics card with DirectX 9 (or above) or OpenGL support

- .NET 2.0 for text import filters (Word 2007/2010 + OpenOffice) (installed by default)

- Internet account and connection required for Web Publishing features and accessing online resources

First-time install

To install PagePlus X5 simply insert the PagePlus X5 Program DVD into your DVD drive. The AutoRun feature automatically starts the Setup process. Just answer the on-screen questions to install the program.

Re-install

To re-install the software or to change the installation at a later date, select **Settings/Control Panel** from the Windows Start menu and then click on the **Add/Remove Programs** icon. Make sure the PagePlus X5 Program DVD is inserted into your CD drive, click the **Install...** button and then simply follow the on-screen instructions.

2 Getting Started

Startup Wizard

On program launch, the Startup Wizard is displayed which offers different routes into PagePlus:

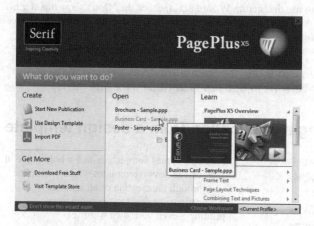

- **Start New Publication**, to open a blank page to work on.

- **Use Design Template**, to create an instant document from a pre-designed template.

- **Import PDF**, to create a publication from an existing PDF.

- **Get More**, to access a range of free resources and design templates (purchasable).

- **Open**, to access recently opened publications. Hover over each entry for a quick preview!

- **Learn**, to access online tutorial resources (web and video).

Use the **Choose Workspace** drop-down menu to choose your workspace appearance (i.e., Studio tab positions, tab sizes, and show/hide tab status). You can adopt the default workspace profile **<Default Profile>**, the last used profile **<Current Profile>**, a range of profile presets, or a workspace profile you have previously saved.

As you select different profiles from the menu, your workspace will preview each tab layout in turn.

The Startup Wizard is displayed by default when you launch PagePlus. If you don't want to use the Startup Wizard again, check the "Don't show this wizard again" box. You can switch it on again via the **Use startup wizard** check box in **Tools>Options...** (use Options>General menu option).

You can also access the Startup Wizard at any time from **New>New from Startup Wizard...** on the **File** menu.

Creating a publication from a design template

Pro Template Packs
Address Labels
Brochures
Business Cards
Business Forms
Calendars
Certificates
Compliment Slips
CVs
Discs
Envelopes
Flyers
Greetings Cards
Invitations
Letterheads
Logos

PagePlus comes complete with a whole range of categorized design templates which will speed you through the creation of all kinds of publications for desktop or commercial printing—even your own website!

Templates also help ensure continuity between your pages by preserving such elements as page layout, contents, styles, and colour palettes. They also offer quality pictures that you can use royalty free.

Theme Layouts
- ⊞ Editorial
- ⊞ Graphical
- ⊞ Illustrative
- ⊟ Textured
  - Clouds
  - Doodle
  - Eco
  - Good Morning
  - Industrial
  - Ledger
  - Nature
  - Paper Office
  - Pop
  - Shabby
  - Vintage
  - Zine

Instead of a design template, you can adopt a **Theme Layout** instead; layouts offer picture placeholders instead of actual pictures. Different physical document types (Brochure, Business Card, Flyer, Forms, Letterheads, Newsletter, etc.) can be created from a categorized theme (e.g., Textured category, Eco theme layout below), each type offering a choice of complementary multiple page designs.

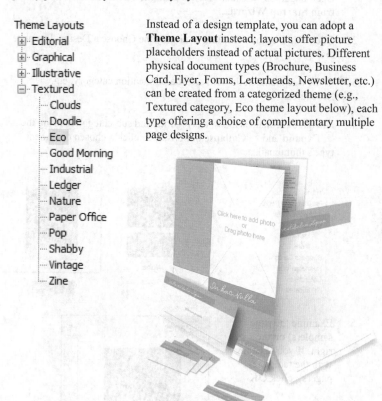

Once selected, the publication is normally all but complete apart from adding your own pictures to placeholders, personalizing placeholder text, or fine-tuning object positioning.

To create a publication from a design template:

1. Open PagePlus, or choose **New...** from the **File** menu and select **New from Startup Wizard...**.

2. Click **Use Design Template** to display the Choose a Design Template dialog.

3. In the tree menu on the left, select a publication category, e.g. Brochures.

4. Navigate the main window's categories and sub-categories using the ⊞ **Expand** and ⊟ **Collapse** buttons, then click a chosen document type's thumbnail.

5. Examine the page sample(s) on the right. If you're happy with the template page(s), click **OK**.

To create a publication from a themed layout:

1. From the dialog's Templates list, select **Theme Layouts**, then choose a theme layout category and then a theme name from the list.

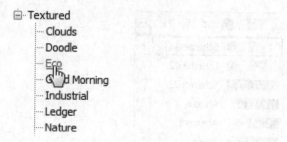

2. The adjacent pane updates to show document types for that selected theme. Select a thumbnail.

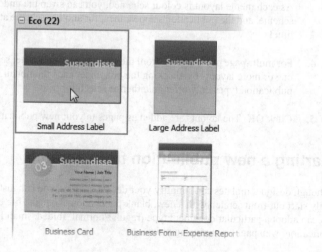

3. In the upper-right corner of the dialog, choose a document colour scheme on which to base your publication from the drop-down list (the first three schemes are designed specifically for the chosen themed layout).

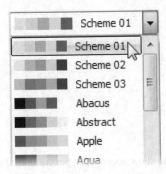

As each theme layout is colour schemed, you can swap the underlying scheme, and the publication's appearance, for another scheme at any time!

4. For multi-page publications, from the right-hand Pages pane, select one or more layouts by checking the box under each thumbnail. Some publication types only offer an either/or selection.

5. Click **OK**. The layouts are added as pages to your new publication.

Starting a new publication from scratch

Although design templates can simplify your design choices, you can just as easily start out from scratch with a new, blank publication. To make life easier you can adopt a particular document type (regular/normal, folded, small/large publication, web page) as a starting point.

To start a new publication (via Startup Wizard):

1. Open PagePlus to display the initial Startup Wizard (if switched on).
   - or -
   With PagePlus loaded, choose **New...** from the **File** menu and then select **New from Startup Wizard...**.

2. Select **Start New Publication**.

3. From the list on the left, select a document type and then examine the samples on the right. Click the sample that is the closest match to the document you want to create.
- or -
You can define a custom publication by clicking **Custom Page Setup...**.

4. Click **OK** to open a new publication with a blank page.

At start up, if you click  (or press **Escape**) from the Startup Wizard, PagePlus opens a blank document using default page properties.

To start a new default publication:

- Click ⬜ **New Publication** on the **Standard** toolbar (only if Startup Wizard is turned off).

Opening existing publications

You can open a PagePlus publication from the Startup Wizard, **Standard** toolbar, or via the **File** menu.

It is also possible to open PDF files as new publications, or Import PDF files and existing PagePlus files into currently open publications. (See PagePlus Help for both of these import options.)

To open an existing publication from the Startup Wizard:

1. From the Startup Wizard (at startup time or via **File>New**), review your publications from the Open section. The most recently opened file will be shown at the top of the list. To see a thumbnail preview of any file before opening, hover over its name in the list.

   Open
   Dive_for_life.ppp
   PolicyPaper.ppp
   GetHighClimbing
   ClassicHouses.pp
   Environ_345.ppp
   EternityPearls.pp
   scrapbook.ppp

2. Click the file name to open it.

   Dive_for_life.ppp

⚝ If your publication hasn't been opened recently, click 🗁 **Browse...** to navigate to it.

⚝ Recently viewed files also appear at the bottom of the File menu. Simply select the file name to open it.

To open existing publications from within PagePlus:

1. Click 🗁 **Open** on the **Standard** toolbar.

2. In the **Open** dialog, select the folder and file name(s). For multiple publications, **Shift**-click to select adjacent multiple files or **Ctrl**-click to select non-adjacent files.

3. Click the **Open** button.

To open publications by drag-and-drop:

• From Windows Explorer, drag and drop an image file or preview thumbnail anywhere onto the PagePlus workspace.

To revert to the saved version of an open publication:

• Choose **Revert** from the **File** menu.

Font substitution

PagePlus supports automatic and manual font substitution if you open a publication which uses fonts which are not stored on your computer. See PagePlus Help for more details.

Working with more than one publication

If you have multiple publications open at the same time it's easy to jump between them using different methods.

Click on an open publication's tab on the **Publications** toolbar at the top of the workspace to make it active (e.g., p456).

Alternatively, you can select the name of a currently open publication from the **Window** menu. Unsaved publications are indicated by an asterisk; the currently active publication is shown with a tick.

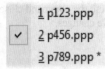

Saving your publication

To save your work:

- Click **Save** on the **Standard** toolbar.

- To save under a different name, choose **Save As...** from the **File** menu.

Unsaved publications have an asterisk after their name in either the PagePlus title bar or **Window** menu.

Closing publications

To close the current publication:

- On the active publication's Publication tab, click the  **Close** button.

- or -
Choose **Close** from the **File** menu.
- or -
If the publication is in a cascaded/tiled window, click the window's
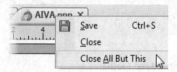 **Close** button.
- or -
If it's the only window open for the publication, the command closes
the publication and you'll be prompted to save changes.

To close all publications except current:

- Right click a Publication tab and choose **Close All But This**. You'll be
prompted to save changes for any unsaved publication.

To close PagePlus:

- Click the program's ![X] **Close** button at the top right of the
window.

You'll be prompted to save changes to any unsaved publications.

Updating and saving defaults

Object defaults are the stored property settings PagePlus applies to *newly created objects* such as:

- **lines** and **shapes** (line and fill colour, shade, pattern, transparency, etc.)

- **frames** (margins, columns, etc.)

- **text** (i.e., font, size, colour, alignment, etc.). Defaults are saved separately for **artistic, shape**, **frame** and **table text.**

You can easily change the defaults for any type of object via the **Update Object Default** command or the **Text Style Palette** dialog.

Default settings are always **local**—that is, any changed defaults apply to the current publication and are automatically saved with it, so they're in effect next time you open that publication. However, at any time you can use the **Save Defaults** command to record the current defaults as **global** settings that will be in effect for any new publication you subsequently create.

To set local defaults for a particular type of object:

1. Create a single sample object and fine-tune its properties as desired— or use an existing object that already has the right properties. (For graphics, you can use a line, shape, or rectangle; all share the same set of defaults.)

2. Select the object that's the basis for the new defaults and choose **Update Object Default** from the **Format** menu.

Or, for line and fill colours, including line styles:

1. With no object selected, choose the required line and/or fill colours from the Colour or Swatches tab. Use the Line tab to set a default line weight, style, and corner shape.

2. Draw your object on the page, which will automatically adopt the newly defined default colours and styles.

To view and change default text properties:

1. Choose **Text Style Palette...** from the **Format** menu.

2. Click **Default Text**, then from the expanded list of text types, choose an option (e.g., Artistic Text).

3. Click **Modify...** to view current settings for the selected text type.

4. Use the Text Style dialog to alter character, paragraph, or other properties.

To save all current defaults as global settings:

1. Choose **Save Defaults** from the **Tools** menu.

2. From the dialog, check options to update specific defaults globally:

    - **Document and object defaults** - saves current document settings (page size, orientation) and object settings (context toolbar settings).

    - **Text styles** - saves current text styles in the Text Style Palette.

    - **Object styles** - saves user-defined styles from Styles tab.

    - **Table and calendar formats** - saves custom formats saved in Table Formats dialog.

3. Click **Save** to confirm that you want new publications to use the checked object's defaults globally.

3 Working with Pages

Setting up a publication

A publication's **page size** and **orientation** settings are fundamental to your layout, and are defined when the new publication is first created, either using a design template or as a New Publication choice via **File>New...** and the Startup Wizard. If the Startup Wizard is turned off, or you cancel the setup dialog, a new publication is created to a default page size.

To adjust size/orientation of the current publication:

1. Select ⊞ **Page Setup** from the Pages context toolbar.

2. For a **Regular/Booklet Publication**, you can select a pre-defined paper size, printer-derived paper size, or enter custom values for page **Width** and **Height**, as well as setting the orientation (Portrait or Landscape). For booklets only, select a type from the **Booklet** drop-down menu, which page to start on (left/right), and if you require **Facing pages** (including **Dual master pages**).

    PagePlus automatically performs **imposition**) . The settings ensure that two or four pages of the publication are printed on each sheet of paper, with pages printed following the booklet sequence. This saves you from having to calculate how to position and collate pairs of pages on a single larger page, and lets you use automatic page numbering for the booklet pages.

3. For other publication types, you can select the publication types: **Small Publications** (for example, business cards, labels, etc.), **Large Publications** (banners or posters), or **Folded Publications** (cards).

    *   For Small publications, enable **Paper** and choose a pre-defined option from the list, or for creating **Labels**, enable the radio button and pick an Avery label code which matches your labels.

    *   For Large and Folded publications, choose a pre-defined option from the list (use the preview).

4. Click **OK** to accept the new dimensions. The updated settings will be applied to the current publication.

For regular/booklet publications, you can also adopt printer-derived paper sizes that are supported by your desktop or network printer. These paper sizes are shown in the **Page Setup** dialog and will be different depending on which printer is currently chosen in the Print dialog. On the Pages context toolbar, these page sizes are indicated by the suffix "(From printer)" in the Paper size drop-down menu.

Once you've set up your publication, you can optionally include repeated page elements on every page by creating master pages (p. 38).

Creating custom publication sizes

If the pre-defined options are not what you're looking for, you can customize any publication type to suit your requirements. You can base the custom publication on a pre-defined option by selecting the option in advance from the list.

Created from:	You'll need to:
Regular/Booklet	For regular publications: Select a page size, if you want Facing pages (with Dual master pages) and adjust Width/Height to suit; enable your preferred page orientation option (Portrait/Landscape).
	For booklets: As above, but choose a Booklet type as well.
Small	Select a Small publication type (card, tag, voucher, etc.), then click **Create Custom**. From the dialog, you can set:
	• Size: The custom publication size.
	• Gaps: The vertical and horizontal space between each "ganged" small publication.
	• Margins: For custom Margins, override auto settings with Auto check box and set margins manually.
	• Layout: Sets the number or small publications per page in an X/Y grid arrangement.

> ✎ You never set the size of your small
> publication, instead you control the
> layout and gap size within the set
> publication size.

Large As for Small. Tile Overlap controls the how much printed pages overlap when output to standard printers.

Folded Select a folding method from the list, then choose Width/Height for your publication size.

Facing pages

You can set up your regular publication or booklet so that the PagePlus window displays pages either singly or in pairs—as two facing pages side by side. You'll need facing pages if you're creating a publication where you need to see both the left-hand (verso) and right-hand (recto) pages, or one that employs double-page spreads where a headline or other element needs to run from the left-hand page to the right-hand page.

If you set up a publication to use facing pages, you can specify either a **single** or **dual** master page. A single master page is (as the name implies) a single page; a dual master page is a spread with both a left- and right-page component, allowing you to run elements across the spread in the background of the publication, or position left-side page numbers and right-side page numbers at opposite corners. The Pages tab shows single master pages with a standard page thumbnail, and dual master pages with a split-page thumbnail.

To set up facing pages:

1. In the **Page Setup** dialog, check **Facing Pages**.

2. If you plan to use background elements that span a double-page spread, select **Dual master pages**. This will let you define master pages with paired "left page" and "right page" components.
   - or -
   For a facing-page layout where both left and right pages initially share the same master page, and you don't need to run background elements across the spread, clear **Dual master pages**.

Uniform and mixed page orientations

If you've changed your mind about the page orientation chosen at page setup, you can change the page orientation uniformly across your publication at any time.

PagePlus also lets you create a publication possessing a mixture of portrait and landscape page orientations. Changing a page's portrait orientation to landscape is especially useful when presenting a wide table, calendar, bar chart, or other graph.

To change all publication pages from portrait to landscape (or vice versa):

- From the Pages context toolbar, click the down arrow on the **Publication orientation** button, then select **Landscape Publication** (or **Portrait Publication**) from the flyout.

To change a page from portrait to landscape (or vice versa):

1. In the Pages tab, double-click to select a page.

2. Click **Change page orientation** to swap between portrait and landscape orientation.

   - or -

   From the Pages context toolbar, click the down arrow on the **Page orientation** button, then select **Landscape Page** (or **Portrait Page**) from the flyout.

You can repeat the procedure for any other selected page.

When printing to desktop printers or publishing as PDF, all pages automatically orient themselves to the currently selected printer's orientation. For press-ready PDF output, ensure **Impose pages** is checked in the Publish PDF dialog (General tab). For screen PDF versions, Impose pages can be unchecked to maintain the original orientation of all pages.

⟍   You can also change the orientation of master pages using the equivalent **Change page orientation** on the Pages tab's Master Pages window.

⟍   This feature is only applicable for publications using standard page sizes (e.g., A4, A5, Letter, etc.)

⟍   For multi-page spreads, it's not possible to rotate an individual page within that spread.

Adding, removing, and rearranging pages

Use the **Pages tab** to add/delete standard or master pages, assign master pages to standard pages, and rearrange standard pages using drag-and-drop. You can also change page orientations (see p. 36).

The tab displays master pages in the upper **Master Pages** window (shown collapsed) and standard publication pages in the lower **Pages** window.

The 🗎 **Page Manager** button provides additional options, such as duplicating a particular page or adding/deleting multiple pages.

To add a single page:

1. On the **Pages** tab, click once to select a page in the **Pages** window. The thumbnail that's shown as "selected" is independent of the page you're currently working on. To work on a particular page, double-click its thumbnail.

2. Click 🗎 **Add** to add a page (or master page) *before* the one selected in the window.
   - or -
   To add a new page *at the end* of the publication, deselect all pages by clicking in the neutral region of the lower window, then click the **Add** button.

To add master pages:

For master pages, the above procedure applies but within the Master Pages window.

To delete a single page/master page:

1. On the **Pages** tab, select the page (or master page) to delete on the appropriate window by clicking its thumbnail.

2. Click the ⊟ **Remove** button.

To rearrange pages:

- On the **Pages** tab, in the lower **Pages** window, drag a page thumbnail to a new location in the page sequence.

Understanding master pages

Master pages provide a flexible way to store background elements that you'd like to appear on more than one page—for example a logo, background, header/footer, or border design.

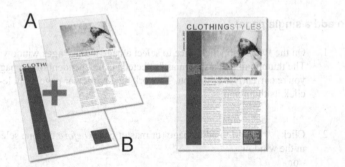

A - Page, B - Master Page

The key concept here is that a particular master page is typically **shared** by multiple pages, as illustrated below. By placing a design element on a master page and then assigning several pages to use that master page, you ensure that all the pages incorporate that element. Of course, each individual page can have its own "foreground" elements.

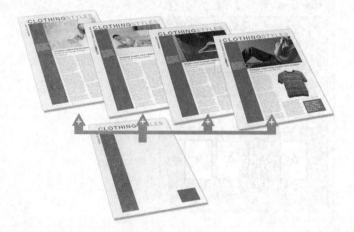

Master pages are available in every publication, but in a simple publication you may not need to use any master pages—or you may need only one master page. Facing pages and multiple master pages prove valuable with longer, more complex publications.

 If you're starting with a design template you may encounter one or more master pages incorporated with the design.

Using the **Pages** tab or **Page Manager**, you can quickly add or delete master pages; for example, you could set up different master pages for "title" or "chapter divider" pages.

Assigning master pages

If you're only using one master page it is assigned to any newly created page by default. However, if you're using multiple master pages you can assign a different master page to a standard page, all, odd or even pages. It's even possible to assign multiple master pages per page.

To assign a master page:

1. From the expanded Master Pages window in the Pages tab, drag a master page onto a target standard page in the lower window.

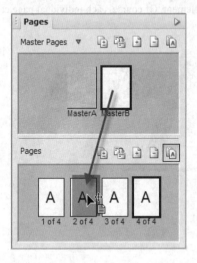

- or –

1. From the Layers tab, right-click a master layer and choose **Set Master Page...**.

2. Select the page and the master page to be assigned to it.

> Click **Show Master Page Identifiers** to indicate the master page (A, B, C, etc.) used on the currently selected page(s).

To assign a master page to odd, even, or all pages:

- In the Pages tab, right-click the master page and select from the **Apply to** submenu.

To disconnect a previously assigned master page(s):

- In the Pages tab, right-click in the Pages window and select **Remove Master Pages**.

Assigning multiple master pages

Just like a regular page, the master page can have its own set of layers associated with it, completely unique from the regular page! From the Layers tab, you'll see a master layer (e.g., Master Layer 1 [A]) as a separate entry. You can insert master layers from other master pages to assign additional master pages to your page. You'll need to create an additional master page first! See p. 37.

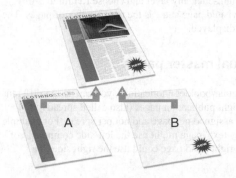

For an introduction to the concept of layers, see Working with layers on p. 47.

To assign multiple master pages to a page:

1. On the Layers tab, select ⬚ **Add Master Layer**.

2. From the dialog's drop-down menu, select the additional master page to be assigned. You'll need to create it first!

3. (Optional) Enter a different name for your layer.

4. You can also modify layer properties as for standard layers.

5. Click **OK**.

To jump to a master page from the standard page:

- Double-click on a Master Layer entry in the Layers tab.
  - or -
  Right-click a master layer and choose **Go To Master Page**.

The master page assigned to the master layer is displayed.

An easy method for navigating from the selected master page to a last visited page is the **Return to** feature.

To jump to a page from a master page:

1. Select the master page in the Pages tab.

2. In the Layers tab, right-click any layer and choose Return to '*x* of *y*', where *x* is the last visited page and *y* is the total number of pages. The last visited page is displayed.

Facing pages and dual master pages

If you're using multi-page regular/booklet publications, you can assign different master pages to the left and right publication pages (also called spreads) if necessary—master pages are assigned per page and not per spread. For example (see below), a left-hand "body text" page might use the left-side component of one master page (**A**), while a right-hand page could use the right side of a different master page (**B**).

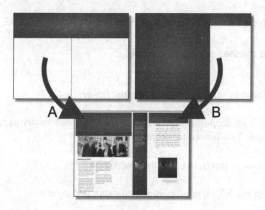

Editing master page objects

If you're editing pages which use master pages, master page objects will contribute to your page design. These objects can be edited quickly and easily from the page by using a control bar under the selected object.

To edit the master page object:

1. On your standard page, select the master page object, to reveal the control bar.

2. Click  **Edit on Master Page**. The master page is displayed for editing.

On occasion, you may want to make a master page object on your page independent from its master page. These objects can become editable by being **promoted** from the master page to the standard page, with the original master page object being replaced by a freely editable copy.

To promote a master page object:

1. On your standard page, select the master page object, to reveal the control bar under the object.

2. Click **Promote from Master Page**. This makes a copy of the original object, which can then be edited independently without affecting the master page.

> All other pages using the master page will remain unaffected.

> Detaching a specific text frame will also detach any linked text frame associated with it. If the frames are on separate pages then all linked frames are placed on the same the target page.

If you change your mind at any point you can reattach the object to the master page, leaving your page as it was originally.

To reattach object:

1. On your standard page, select the promoted object, to reveal the control bar under the object.

2. Click 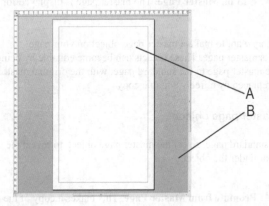 **Revert to Master Page**.

Viewing pages

Most of the PagePlus display is taken up by a page or "artwork" area and a surrounding "pasteboard" area.

A

B

In PagePlus, the **Page** area (A) is where you put page layout guides, and of course the text, shapes, and pictures that you want to print. The **Pasteboard** area (B) is where you generally keep any text, shapes, or pictures that are being prepared or waiting to be positioned on the page area.

To move or copy an object between pages via the Pasteboard:

1. Drag the object from the source page onto the pasteboard (hold down the **Ctrl** key to copy).

2. Use the page navigation buttons on the Hintline to jump to a target page.

3. Drag (or **Ctrl**-drag to copy) the object from the pasteboard onto the target page.

PagePlus makes it easy to see exactly what you're working on—from a wide view of multiple pages to a close-up view of a small region. For example, you can use the **scroll bars** at the right and bottom of the main window to move the page and pasteboard with respect to the main window. If you're using a **wheel mouse**, you can scroll vertically by rotating the wheel, or horizontally by **Shift**-scrolling.

Magnifying pages

For magnification options, the **View** toolbar provides the:

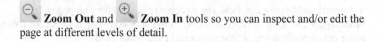 **Zoom Out** and **Zoom In** tools so you can inspect and/or edit the page at different levels of detail.

59% 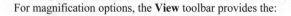 **Zoom Percent** option to set a level of magnification (expressed as a percentage).

Zoom Tool to zoom into an area defined by a drawn marquee selection.

Pan Tool for moving the page area by dragging.

Actual size option for viewing the page at its true size (100%).

Zoom to selection option to focus on a selected area.

Page Width option to fit to the page's width.

Full Page option to fit the page into your current window.

Multi-page option to view multiples pages simultaneously (set page number by dragging a page array from the flyout menu).

Switching view modes

You can switch between different view modes, which offer single or multiple pages to view:

- **Normal** view, which displays one page at a time.

- **Multi-page** view, used for inspecting long documents, displays a number of pages according to a configurable page array (e.g., a 3x1 grid).

In Normal and Multi-page view, the pasteboard is shared by all pages. In Multipage view, it's also especially easy to move or copy objects between pages using drag-and-drop and set the number of pages displayed.

To view multiple pages (in Multi-page mode):

1. Click the ⊞ **Multi-page** flyout on the **View** toolbar. An array selector appears.

2. Click and drag to choose an array within the selector, for example 2 x 4 Pages or 3 x 1 Pages (as shown). To expand the number of choices, drag down and to the right. Click **Normal View** if you change your mind.

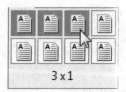

The publication appears in Multi-page mode with the specified page array in view.

To switch between views:

- Choose between **Normal** or **Multi-page** from the **View** menu.

Navigating pages

To switch between pages:

- Click the ◀ **Previous Page**, ▶ **Next Page**, ◀ **First Page** or ▶|
  Last Page button on the Hintline.
  - or -
  Click in the **Current Page** box (e.g., `2 of 4`) and type the
  page number you want to jump to.
  - or -
  On the Studio's **Pages tab**, double-click the page's thumbnail for the
  page (or master page) you want to view. The lower Pages window of
  the tab displays normal pages, while the expandable Master Pages
  window shows only master pages.

To switch between current page and its master page:

- From the Hintline toolbar, click 🔲 **Master Pages**.

Working with layers

When you create a new publication from scratch or from a design template, the
page(s) you create will initially consist of two **layers**—one for the page (Layer
1) and one for the associated master page (see p. 38), e.g., Master Layer 1 [A].
The layers can be seen within a hierarchical stack on the **Layers tab**.

One layer may be enough to accommodate the elements of a particular layout,
but you can create additional layers as needed for the page. Layers are useful
when you're working on a complex design where it makes sense to separate one
cluster of objects from another. You can work on one layer at a time without
worrying about affecting elements on a different layer.

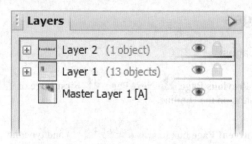

If you frequently use the pasteboard, you'll notice pasteboard objects show under a special Pasteboard layer. This layer automatically disappears when you clear objects off the pasteboard.

A useful feature of the Layers tab is that you can see objects (and grouped objects) under the layer on which they were created. By expanding the layer by clicking ⊞, these objects are displayed—with a click, they can be selected on the page.

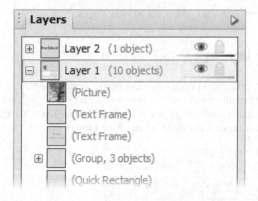

On each layer, objects such as text frames and pictures are stacked in the order you create them, from front to back, with each new object in front of the others. Layers themselves are stacked in a similar way, and of course you can juggle the order of objects and layers as needed. The uppermost layer is applied over any lower layer on the page.

Once you've displayed a page, you can normally edit any object on it— regardless of which layer the object is on—simply by clicking the object.

In order to create new objects on a particular layer, you'll need to select the layer.

To select a particular layer:

- Click a layer name. The layer entry then possesses a dark blue background.

The Master Layer entries work slightly differently to other layers. They indicate firstly that a master page and its layers are being used on the page, but also show the actual master page being used (MasterA is represented by the letter A on the layer entry). The master page's layers are not shown individually, but are combined into one thumbnail for clarity. However, you can display master page layers if required.

To display master page layers:

- Double-click the master layer entry. The Layers tab now shows the master page's layers. Note that the master page is now selected in the Pages tab.

For more information about master pages and assigning them to pages, see Understanding master pages on p. 38.

Adding, removing, and rearranging layers

Once you've created a page, it's easy to add, delete, move, or merge layers as needed. Moving a layer will place its objects in the front or back of those on other layers.

To add a new layer to the current page or master page:

1. In the Layers tab, click ✛ **Add Layer**.

2. You'll be prompted to give the new layer a name and set its properties. When you've made your selections, click **OK**.

The new layer is inserted above the currently selected layer, and is the foremost layer. If a layer is not selected, the new layer is placed at the top of the stack.

To delete a layer:

- In the Layers tab, select the layer's name and click ▭ **Delete Selected Layers**.

You can also move layers, as well as merge, preview, or view only layers. (See PagePlus Help for more details.)

Layer names and properties

The Layers tab lets you rename layers and set a variety of properties for one or more layers.

To rename the layer:

1. In the Layers tab, click on the layer's name.

2. At the insertion point, type a new name then either press **Enter** or click away from the tab.

To set layer properties:

- Display the Layers tab.

Select desired settings for the selected layer.

- Click the 👁 **Visible** icon to hide the layer and any objects on it; click again to reveal the layer.

- Click the 🖶 **Printable** icon to exclude the layer in page printouts; click again to include it. At print time, uncheck the **Print all layers** option in the Print dialog (Layers menu option) to exclude non-printable layers.

- Click the 🔒 **Locked** icon to prevent objects on the layer from being selected/edited; click again to allow editing.

🖈 You cannot select objects on a layer that is locked or not visible.

Double-click a layer or click ⬚ **Layer properties** to change selection handle colour and extend settings to layers with the same name. See Layers tab in PagePlus Help.

Copying layers and objects

When you add a new page or master page to the publication, you can specify whether to copy the layers, objects, and/or the master page from a particular source page. See Adding, removing, and rearranging pages on p. 37.

Managing objects on layers

Objects can be managed in the Layers tab with various options for selecting, moving, and naming them.

Once you've displayed a page or master page, you can normally select and then edit any object on it—regardless of which layer the object is on—simply by clicking the object. Alternatively, you can limit object selection and editing to objects on a specific layer.

To edit only objects on the selected layer:

- In the Layers tab, select the chosen layer and click ✎ **Edit All Layers**.

PagePlus also gives you the option of selecting an object from the tab as opposed to from the page itself.

To select an object on a particular layer:

- In the Layers tab, click the ⊞ **Expand** on the chosen layer entry to reveal all associated objects. You'll see objects named automatically, e.g. "Line", "Picture", "Quick Rectangle", etc., each with their own preview (hover over for a magnified view). The frontmost object in your drawing always appears at the top of the layer's listed objects (the order reflects the Z-order).

To select all objects on a particular layer:

- In the Layers tab, right-click the chosen layer and choose **Select Objects**.

To move an object to a specific layer:

- Drag the object to a new position in the layer stack.
  - or -
  Select the object and choose **Send to Layer** from the **Arrange** menu (or the right-click Arrange submenu), then select the destination layer from the submenu.

Objects are given default names when they are created (e.g., Text Frame, Picture), but can be renamed to make them more easy identify them from other layer objects. If a group is present it can also be assigned a more meaningful name.

To change an object's or group's name:

1. In the Layers tab, expand the layer entry to which an object or group belongs.

2. Select the object/group, then click on its name.

3. At the insertion point, type a new name then either press **Enter** or click away from the tab.

Setting guides

Layout guides are visual guide lines that help you position layout elements. They can include **page margins**, **row and column guides**, **bleed area guides**, and **ruler guides**.

Page margin settings are fundamental to your layout, and usually are among the first choices you'll make after starting a publication from scratch. The page margins are shown as a blue box which is actually four guide lines—for top, bottom, left, and right—indicating the underlying page margin settings. If you like, you can set the margins to match your current printer settings.

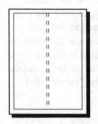

You also have the option of setting up **row** and **column guides** as an underlying layout aid. PagePlus represents rows and columns on the page area with dashed blue guide lines. Unlike the dashed grey frame margins and columns, row and column guides don't control where frame text flows. Rather, they serve as visual aids that help you match the frame layout to the desired column layout.

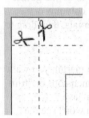

Bleed area guides assist you in positioning "bleed" elements that you want to run to the edge of a trimmed page. To allow for inaccuracies in the trimming process in professional printing, it's a good idea to extend these elements beyond the "trim edge"—the dimensions defined by your Page Setup. With bleed guides switched on, the page border expands by a distance you specify, and the trim edge is shown with dashed lines and little "scissors" symbols. Note that these guide lines are just a visual aid; only the Bleed limit setting in the Publish as PDF or Print dialog extends the actual output page size.

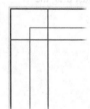

Ruler guides are free-floating lines that you set by clicking and dragging from the rulers. They are "sticky" so that objects can snap to them, then be moved collectively with guide movement.

Defining layout guides

To define layout guides:

*   Click [⊞] **Layout Guides** on the Page context toolbar, **Layout Guides...** from the **File** menu, or right-click on a blank part of the page and choose **Layout Guides**. Then in the **Layout Guides** dialog, use the **Margins** tab to set guide lines for page margins, rows and columns, and bleed areas.

- In the **Margin Guides** section, you can set the left, right, top, and bottom page margins individually, or click the **From Printer** button to derive the page margin settings from the current printer settings. The dialog also provides options for **Balanced margins** (left matching right, top matching bottom) or for **Mirrored margins** on facing pages where the "left" margin setting becomes the "inside," and the "right" margin becomes the "outside."

- Use the **Row and Column Guides** section to define guides for rows and columns. If you want rows or columns of uneven width, first place them at fixed intervals, then drag to reposition them as required.

- Use **Bleed area guides** to specify the extra margin you want to allow around the original Page Setup dimensions or "trim area." Note that if the setting is zero or you have **View>Bleed Area Guides** unchecked, you won't see the bleed area displayed.

- For ruler guides, use the **Guides** tab to precisely create, edit or delete ruler guides, or more commonly, just drag the guides from the rulers.

To show or hide guides:

- On the **View** menu, check or uncheck a guide option.

Creating ruler guides

PagePlus lets you to set up horizontal and vertical **ruler guides**—non-printing lines you can use to align headlines, pictures, and other layout elements.

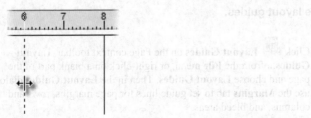

Guides are by default "sticky" so that stuck objects can be dragged around the page by their ruler guide—a great way to move previously aligned objects in bulk and simultaneously.

- To create a ruler guide, click on a ruler, hold down your mouse button, then drag onto your page. A ruler guide line appears parallel to the ruler (**Alt**-drag to create the guide at 90 degrees to the ruler).

- To move a guide, drag it.

- To remove a guide, drag and drop it anywhere outside the page area.

- For precise ruler guide placement, check **Ruler marks** in **Tools>Options>Layout** to snap guides to ruler marks.

- To unstick a selected object, click one of two small red triangular markers shown at the point where the object is attached to the guide. You'll see a link cursor (⬤) as you hover over the sticky guide marker.

- To turn sticky guides on and off, check/uncheck **Sticky Guides** from the **Arrange** menu (or the equivalent from **Tools>Options>Layout**). Previously stuck objects will remain sticky even after sticky guides are switched off—you'll have to make them non-sticky manually.

Using the rulers and dot grid

The PagePlus **rulers** mimic the paste-up artist's T-square, and serve several purposes:

- To act as a measuring tool.

- To create ruler guides for aligning and snapping.

- To set and display tab stops (see p. 120).

- To set and display paragraph indents (see p. 119).

Ruler units

To select the basic measurement unit used by the rulers:

- Right-click the 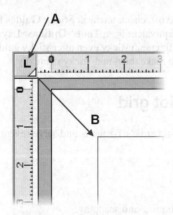 Ruler Intersection and set the measurement unit from the flyout.

In Paper Publishing mode, the default unit is inches (US) or centimetres (international); in Web Publishing mode, only pixels can be used.

Adjusting rulers

By default, the horizontal ruler lies along the top of the PagePlus window and the vertical ruler along the left edge. The default **ruler intersection** is the top-left corner of the pasteboard area. The default **zero point** (marked as 0 on each ruler) is the top-left corner of the page area. (Even if you have set up bleed area guides and the screen shows an oversize page, the zero point stays in the same place, i.e. the top-left corner of the trimmed page.)

(A) Ruler intersection; (B) drag tab marker to set new zero point.

To define a new zero point:

- Drag the tab marker on the ruler intersection to a new zero point on the page or pasteboard. (Be sure to click only the triangular marker!)

To move the rulers:

- With the **Shift** key down, drag the tab marker on the ruler intersection.
  The zero point remains unchanged.

- Double-click on the ruler intersection to make the rulers and zero
  point jump to the top left-hand corner of the currently selected object.
  This comes in handy for measuring page objects.

To restore the original ruler position and zero point:

- Double-click the tab marker on the ruler intersection.

To lock the rulers and prevent them from being moved:

- Choose **Tools>Options...** and select the **Layout>Rulers** page, then
  check **Lock Rulers**.

Rulers as a measuring tool

The most obvious role for rulers is as a measuring tool. As you move the mouse
pointer along the ruler, small lines along each ruler display the current
horizontal and vertical cursor position. When you click to select an object,
shaded ruler regions indicate the object's left/right and top/bottom edges on the
horizontal and vertical rulers, respectively. Each region has a zero point relative
to the object's upper left corner, so you can see the object's dimensions at a
glance.

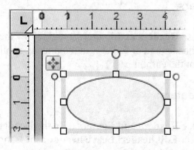

Using the dot grid

The **dot grid** is a matrix of dots based on ruler units, covering the page and pasteboard areas. Like ruler guides, it's handy for both visual alignment and snapping.

- To turn the dot grid on or off, click **Dot Grid** on the **View** menu.

You can also set the grid spacing, style, colour, and positioning in the dialog (see PagePlus Help).

Using headers and footers

Headers and footers are layout elements that are positioned at the top and bottom of your master page(s), and are repeated on every page of your publication. The **Headers and Footers Wizard** lets you create these elements easily.

Remember to set up your margins so that you leave enough room for any intended header or footer.

To create headers and/or footers:

- On the **Insert** menu, choose **Headers and Footers...** and follow the Wizard instructions. The header and/or footer is automatically applied to the master page (and not the current page).

To edit existing headers and footers:

- On the **Insert** menu, choose **Headers and Footers...**. In the **Headers and Footers Wizard**, select **Edit header**, **Leave header as it is**, or **Delete header** and then complete the Wizard instructions. Carry out the equivalent operation for your footer if needed.

Using page numbering

Page number fields automatically display the current page number. Typically, these fields are added automatically to the master page (so they appear on every page) with the Header and Footers Wizard, but you can insert a page number field anywhere in your text.

You can change the style of page numbers, create mixed page number formats, set starting page number(s), and control number continuation across chapters and publication sections (all via **Page Number Format** on the **Format** menu).

To define a header or footer that includes a page number field:

1. Create a header or footer on the master page by choosing **Headers and Footers...** from the **Insert** menu.

2. In the wizard, press the **Page Number** button to insert a page number field (as a prefix or suffix) along with any optional header/footer text.

3. Complete the wizard.

To insert a page number field:

1. Switch to the master page (if desired) by clicking the Current Page box on the Hintline.

2. With the **Artistic Text Tool** selected (**Tools** toolbar), click for an insertion point to place the page number.

3. On the **Insert** menu, select **Page Number** from the **Information** flyout.

You can also specify the **First Page Number** in the sequence (this will appear on the first page of the publication). For example, Chapter Two of a long publication might be in a separate file and begin numbering with page 33.

To set the first page number:

1. Uncheck **Continue from previous chapter**. PagePlus keeps this checked by default so that number continuation is maintained if your publication is to be part of a book.

2. Enter a different **First Page Number**.

For simple publications, it's likely that the same page format is used (e.g., Arabic numerals throughout). However, for more complex publications, different formats can be used for different page ranges, with each page range belonging to its own **publication section**.

To create mixed page number formats:

1. On the **Format** menu, choose **Page Number Format...**.

2. From the dialog's Section list box, select the page range within which you want to create a new number format.

3. Click **Add**, then enter a page from which to start a new section.

4. With the new section created (and selected), choose a different Style. As an example, you could apply Roman numerals to your Table of Contents pages.

Pages	Format
1 - 2	1 - 2
3 - 6	iii - vi
7 - 89	7 - 89

5. Repeat the process for additional sections. Use **Delete** to remove a selected section.

Each section can have its own starting page number for its page numbering sequence. If the first section is selected, a **Continue from previous chapter** option is shown (if part of a book, the numbering is continued from a previous chapter; otherwise 1 is assumed). For any subsequent selected section, the option **Continue from previous section** is used. This can be unchecked, allowing for independent starting page numbers per section.

4 Working with Objects

Selecting an object

↖ ▾ Before you can change any object, you need to select it using one of a choice of tools. The tools share a common **Selection Tools** flyout on the **Tools** toolbar.

↖ Pointer Tool
Click to use the **Pointer Tool** to select, move, copy, resize or rotate objects.

⌀ Lasso Tool
Click to use the **Lasso Tool** to draw a freeform region under which any objects will become selected.

↻ Rotate Tool
Click to use the **Rotate Tool** to rotate an object around a rotation origin (normally centred). See Rotating an object on p. 77.

Prior to any selection, PagePlus objects will display a "glowing" selection hover highlight around the object. In a complex grouping of objects, this indicates which object will become selected.

To select an object:

- Click on the "glowing" object using one of the tools shown above.

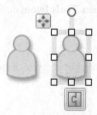

The above example shows an unselected and selected object (showing Move and Group buttons).

If objects overlap, click on the overlapping area until the "hidden" object is selected.

For more precise object selection, you can draw an irregular-shaped lasso around one or more objects in a complex design.

To select an object with the Lasso Tool:

1. Select the **Lasso Tool**.

2. Draw a "lasso" around the object(s) you want to select. A shaded lasso region is created around the object.

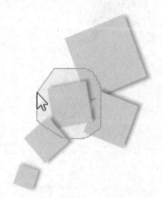

3. Release the mouse button. All of the objects within the lasso region are selected.

If attempting to lasso an object within a group, remember to ungroup the objects first.

To avoid picking up an object under your cursor, keep the **Shift** key pressed as you draw the lasso.

If you prefer to keep the Pointer Tool selected, you can lasso objects as described above with the **Alt** key pressed.

To select a text object with the Pointer Tool:

*   Clicking on a text object (artistic text or text frame) with the Pointer Tool selects the object and also positions the blinking text selection cursor within the object's text. In this mode, you can edit the text (see p. 117).

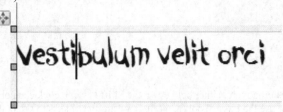

*   Double-, triple-, or quadruple-click to select a word, paragraph, or all text.

*   To select only the text frame, click the frame's bounding box.

*   Clicking on a group selects the grouped object. **Ctrl**-click to select an individual object within a group.

Selecting multiple objects

Selecting more than one object at a time (creating a **multiple selection**) lets you:

- Position or resize all the objects at the same time.

- Create a **group object** from the multiple selection, which can then be treated as a single object, with the option of restoring the individual objects later. See Creating groups on p. 71.

To create a multiple selection:

- Drag a "marquee" box around the objects you want to select.

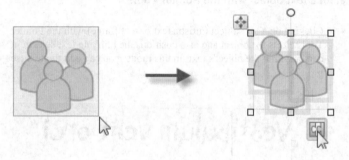

Alternatively, either hold down the **Shift** key and click each object in turn, or use the Lasso Tool (p. 64) to draw around objects to select them.

To add or remove an object from a multiple selection:

- Hold down the **Shift** key and click the object to be added or removed.

To deselect all objects in a multiple selection:

- Click in a blank area of the page.

To select all objects on the page (or master page):

- Choose **Select>Select All** from the **Edit** menu (or press **Ctrl+A**).

- Display the Layers tab, choose the layer name and right-click to **Select Objects**.

Copying, pasting, and replicating objects

Besides using the Windows Clipboard to copy and paste objects, you can duplicate objects easily using drag-and-drop, and replicate multiple copies of any object in precise formations. You can also transfer the formatting of one object to another, with the option of selecting specific attributes to be included when formatting is pasted.

To copy an object (or multiple selection) to the Windows Clipboard:

- Click 📋 **Copy** on the **Standard** toolbar.

If you're using another Windows application, you can usually copy and paste objects via the Clipboard.

To paste an object from the Clipboard:

- Click 📋 **Paste** on the **Standard** toolbar.

The standard Paste command inserts the object at the insertion point or (for a separate object) at the centre of the page. To insert a separate object at the same page location as the copied item, use the **Paste in Place** command.

To choose between alternative Clipboard formats:

- Choose **Paste Special...** from the **Edit** menu.

To duplicate an object:

1. Select the object, then press the **Ctrl** key.

2. Drag the object via the 🔅 **Move** button to a new location on the page, then release the mouse button.

3. To constrain the position of the copy (to same horizontal or vertical), also press and hold down the **Shift** key while dragging. A duplicate of the object appears at the new location.

Replicating objects

Duplicating an object means making just one copy at a time. The **Replicate** command lets you create multiple copies in a single step, with precise control over how the copies are arranged, either as a linear series or a grid. You can include one or more transformations to produce an interesting array of rotated and/or resized objects. It's great for repeating backgrounds, or for perfectly-aligned montages of an image or object.

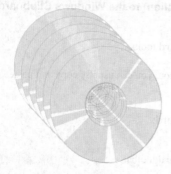

To replicate an object:

1. Select the object to be replicated and choose **Replicate...** from the **Edit** menu. The Replicate dialog appears.

2. To arrange copies in a straight line, select **Create line**. For an X-by-Y grid arrangement, select **Create grid**.

3. Specify **Line length** (the number of objects including the original) in the arrangement, or the Grid size. Note that you can use the Line length setting to include an odd number of objects in a grid.

4. Set spacing between the objects as either an **Offset** (measured between the top left corners of successive objects) or a **Gap** (between the bottom right and top left corners). You can specify **Horizontal** and/or **Vertical** spacing, and/or an angular **Rotation**. To set a specific horizontal or vertical interval, check **Absolute**; uncheck the box to specify the interval as a percentage of the original object's dimensions.

5. Click **OK**.

The result is a multiple selection. Click its ⌗ **Group** button if you want to keep the separate objects linked for additional manipulations.

Pasting an object's formatting

Once you have copied an object to the Clipboard, you can use **Paste Format** (**Edit** menu) to apply its formatting attributes to another object. Again from the **Edit** menu, **Paste Format Plus** displays a "master control" **Style Attributes Editor** dialog that lets you optionally select or deselect specific attributes to be included when formatting is pasted. See Saving object styles on p. 216 for more dialog information.

Snapping

The **snapping** feature simplifies placement and alignment by "magnetizing" moved or resized objects to grid dots and ruler guides. Objects can also snap to other guides on the page such as page margins, rows, columns, and bleeds (see p. 52), as well as the page edge, and page/margin centres (i.e., the centre of the page in relation to the page edge or page margins).

In addition, **dynamic guides** can be used to align and resize objects to existing object edges and centres by snapping. Guides appear dynamically as you drag objects.

To turn snapping on/off globally:

- Click ⌗ ▾ **Snapping** on the Hintline (don't click the drop-down arrow). The button has an orange colour when snapping is switched on.

Once snapping is enabled, you can selectively switch on/off snapping options (i.e., Ruler guides, Grid dots, etc).

To turn individual snapping controls on and off:

- Click the down arrow on the ⌗ ▾ **Snapping** button (Hintline) and check/uncheck a snapping option via the drop-down menu.

> ✎ **Tools>Options** offers the full set of snapping options for the user. You can also control **Snapping Distance**, i.e. the distance at which an object will start to snap to a dot, guide, etc.

> ✎ For precise ruler guide placement, check **Ruler Marks** in **Tools>Options** to snap guides to ruler marks.

Snapping with dynamic guides

For accurate object alignment and resizing, you can use **dynamic guides** instead of setting ruler guides manually or performing selection, transform, and alignment operations. These red-coloured guides are shown between the vertices of the **last three selected** placed page objects and the manipulated object and "visually suggest" possible snapping options such as snap to the placed object's left, right, centre, top, right, bottom, or to the page centre. You can include objects to snap to by dragging over objects.

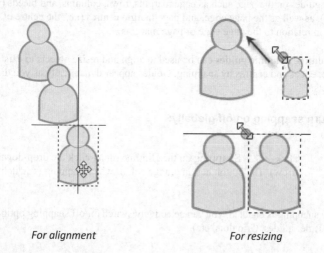

For alignment   *For resizing*

To switch on dynamic guides:

- Click the down arrow on the ⬚▾ **Snapping** button (Hintline) and click **Dynamic Guides** on the drop-down menu.

✎ To snap to page centres as well, you must additionally check **Page centre** in **Tools>Options>Layout>Snapping**.

Creating groups

You can easily turn a multiple selection into a group object. When objects are grouped, you can position, resize, or rotate the objects all at the same time.

To create a group from a multiple selection:

- Click the **Group Objects** button.

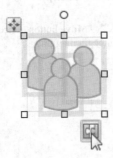

To ungroup:

- Click the **Ungroup Objects** button. The group turns back to a multiple selection.

Simply clicking on any member of a group selects the group object. In general, any operation you carry out on a selected group affects each member of the group. However, the objects that comprise a group are intact, and you can also select and edit an individual object within a group.

To select an individual object within a group:

- **Ctrl**-click the object.

Moving objects

To move an object (including a multiple selection):

- Drag the selected object by using its 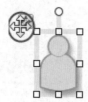 **Move** button. Once you see a move cursor over the button you can begin dragging.

> To set exact horizontal and vertical positions, use the **Transform tab**.

To constrain the movement of an object to horizontal or vertical:

- Select the object and use the keyboard arrows (up, down, left, right).

Resizing objects

PagePlus provides several methods for resizing single or grouped objects. Click-and-drag is the simplest—watch the Hintline for context-sensitive tips and shortcuts!

To resize an object (in general):

1. Select the object.

2. Click one of the selection handles and drag it to a new position while holding down the left mouse button.

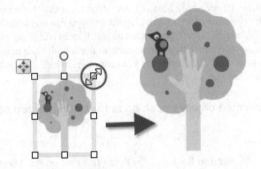

Dragging from an edge handle resizes in one dimension, by moving that edge. Dragging from a corner handle resizes in two dimensions, by moving two edges.

✎ Text in frames and tables doesn't change size when the container object is resized.

✎ To set two or more objects to the same horizontal or vertical size as the last selected object, you can use **Arrange>Size Objects....**

✎ You can also make fine resizing adjustments from the Transform tab.

To resize freely:

• Drag from a corner (or line end) handle.

To constrain a shape, frame object, or table object when resizing:

• Hold the **Shift** key down and drag from a corner (or line end) handle.

For shapes, this has the effect of keeping a square as a square, a circle as a circle, etc.

For pictures, dimensions are constrained on dragging a corner handle. Use **Shift**-drag to resize a picture freely.

Ordering objects

Each new page or master page consists of a single layer; a page with a master page also shows the master page's Master Layer. One layer may be enough to accommodate the elements of a particular layout, but you can create additional layers as needed. On each layer, objects such as text frames and pictures are **stacked** in the order you create them, from back to front, with each new object in front of the others. You can change the stacking order, which affects how objects appear on the page.

To shift the selected object's position to the bottom or top of the stack:

- Click 🔲 **Send to Back** or 🔲 **Bring to Front** on the **Arrange** toolbar, respectively.

To shift the object's position one step toward the back or front:

- Right-click on the object and choose **Arrange>Back One** or **>Forward One**, respectively.

For complete control while ordering objects, the Layers tab lets you drag and drop an object to any position in the stack within the layer, but also to a new position in a different layer.

To order objects via the Layers tab:

- From the Layers tab, drag an object to its new position. A green line indicates the object's new position when you release the mouse button.

Aligning and distributing objects

Alignment involves taking a group of selected objects and aligning them all in one operation by their top, bottom, left or right edges. You can also distribute objects, so that your objects (as a multiple selection) are spread evenly (optionally at spaced intervals).

Alignment or distribution can occur between the endmost objects on your page (current selection), page margins, page edge. For example, with multiple selected objects, aligning to Top, aligns all objects to the topmost edge of the highest object; align to Bottom aligns all objects to the topmost edge of the highest object.

Alignment to last selected object lets you choose a specific object in a multiple selection from which to align other objects.

To align the edges of two or more objects in a selection:

1. Using the Pointer Tool, **Shift**-click on all the objects you want to align, or draw a marquee box around them, to create a multiple selection.

2. Select the Align tab.

3. Select an option for vertical and/or horizontal alignment. Choose **Top**, **Bottom**, **Left**, **Right**, **Centre Horizontally** or **Centre Vertically**, i.e.

To distribute two or more objects across a selection:

- Choose  **Space Evenly Across** or **Space Evenly Down** to spread selected objects uniformly between endmost objects in the current selection (horizontally or vertically, respectively) or by a set measurement (choose **Spaced** and set a value in any measurement unit).

Rather than work within the current selection area you can align or distribute to page margins (if set) or page edge.

To align/distribute objects to page margins, edges, or across page spreads:

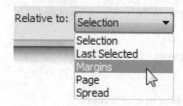

- Select from the **Relative to** drop-down menu to align the selected object(s) within the page **Margins**, **Page** edges, or **Spread** (for facing pages) then choose an align or distribute button described above.

For more advanced alignment control, you can align multiple objects in relation to your last selected object (select objects in turn with the **Shift** key pressed) by using the **Relative to: Last Selected** drop-down list option.

Exporting as a picture

Exporting as a picture lets you convert all the objects on the page, or just the currently selected object(s), to an image file, using a file format you specify.

To export as a picture:

1. (If exporting objects, not the whole page) Select the object or **Shift**-click (or drag a marquee) to select multiple objects.

2. Choose **Export As Picture...** from the **File** menu.

3. In the **Save as type** drop-down list, select a image format, e.g. **Serif MetaFile Format (*.smf)**.

4. Specify a folder and file name for the picture.

5. To export just selected object(s), check **Selected object(s)**. To export the whole page, uncheck this box.

6. To choose from export options such as resolution, colour, and transparency, check **Show filter options**.

7. Click **Save**. You'll see export options, if available and requested, for the particular export filter in use.

Exporting Serif Metafiles

PagePlus lets you export pictures in Serif Metafile Format (SMF). This proprietary format, an improvement on the Windows Metafile Format (WMF) due to improved text, line and fill handling, is especially useful for interworking between Serif products, i.e. you may want to utilize PagePlus objects in another Serif application to save time and effort. The object is converted to a graphic and becomes non-editable, but the object's original appearance will be honoured.

Rotating an object

You can rotate single and multiple objects, including pictures, text objects, and groups using the object's rotation handle or the Rotate Tool.

To rotate a selected object (using its rotation handle):

- Click and drag the rotation handle extending from the selection box (use the **Shift** key while dragging for 15° rotation intervals).

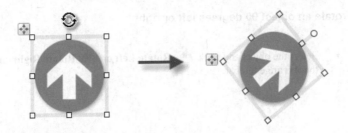

To rotate an object (using Rotate Tool):

1. Select the **Rotate Tool** on the **Tools** toolbar's Selection flyout.

2. Click to select the object, hover over one of its edge or corner handles until you see the rotate cursor.

3. Hold the mouse button down and drag the cursor in the direction in which you want to rotate the object, then release.

The Pointer Tool can also be used to rotate objects in the same way (with the ↻ cursor).

To undo rotation (then restore the original orientation):

- Double-click the object.

- To restore the rotated position, double-click again.

To change the rotation origin:

1. Select the ⟳ **Rotate Tool** and click to select the object.

2. Move the rotation origin ⊕ away from its original position in the centre of the object to any position on the page. The origin can also be moved to be outside the object—ideal for rotating grouped objects around a central point.

3. Drag the rotation handle to a new rotation angle—the object will rotate about the new origin.

To reset the rotation origin, simply double-click it.

To rotate an object 90 degrees left or right:

- Select the object and click ⬔ **Rotate Left** or ⬔ **Rotate Right** on the **Arrange** toolbar.

Flipping an object

You can flip objects horizontally (left to right; top and bottom stay the same) or vertically (top to bottom; left and right stay the same).

To flip an object horizontally/vertically:

- Select the object and choose **Flip Horizontal** or **Flip Vertical** from the **Arrange** menu.

Cropping and combining objects

Cropping means masking (hiding) parts of an object, for example to improve composition or create a special effect. The underlying object remains intact. Two types of cropping are possible—**square** cropping or **irregular** cropping.

square crop   *irregular crop*

Combining starts with more than one object, but creates a special composite object with one or more "holes" on the inside where the component objects' fills overlapped one another—useful for creating mask or stencil effects.

To crop using the object's original outline:

1. Select the object, then select the ⊓ **Square Crop Tool** on the **Attributes** toolbar's Crop flyout.

2. For a vector object (shape, line, etc.), drag one of its edge or corner handles inward for unconstrained cropping; press the **Shift** key while dragging for constrained cropping (aspect ratio is maintained). For pictures (above), the crop operation is constrained by default.

> To scale the object within the crop outline, press the **Ctrl** key, click your left mouse button, then move your mouse upwards or downwards.

To crop by modifying the object's outline:

- Select the object and select the ⊏ **Irregular Crop Tool** on the **Attributes** toolbar's Crop flyout. The Curve context toolbar appears, which lets you control the displayed nodes and connecting segments that define the object's crop outline. See Editing lines in PagePlus Help.

  - To move a node (control point) where you see the ⁻⌐⁻ cursor, drag the node.

  - To move a line segment (between two nodes) where you see the cursor, drag the segment.

To position a cropped object within its crop outline:

- With either crop tool selected, click the object and drag its centre (when you see the hand cursor).

To feather the crop outline:

- With either crop tool selected, click the object.

- From the Crop context toolbar, set a **Feather** value using the up/down arrows, slider or by direct input. Feathering is applied outside the crop outline by the set point size.

To uncrop (restore full visibility):

- Click the 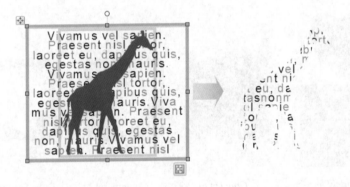 **Remove Crop** button on the **Attributes** toolbar's Crop flyout.

Cropping one shape to another

The **Crop to Shape** command works with exactly two objects selected. Either or both of these may be a group object. The lower object (the one behind the other) gets clipped to the outline of the upper object, leaving a shape equivalent to the overlapping region.

To crop one shape to another:

1. Place the "clipping" object in front of the object to be cropped, using the **Arrange** menu and/or **Arrange** toolbar as needed.

2. With both objects selected (or grouped), choose **Crop to Shape** from the **Tools** menu.

You can restore an object cropped in this way to its original shape, but the upper "cropping" object is permanently deleted (use **Undo** to recover it if necessary).

Combining lines and shapes

Combining curves is a way of creating a composite object from two or more lines or drawn shapes. As with cropping to a shape, the object in front clips the object(s) behind, in this case leaving one or more "holes" where the component objects overlapped. As with grouping, you can apply formatting (such as line or fill) to the combined object and continue to edit individual nodes and segments with the **Pointer Tool**. Unlike those other methods, a combined object permanently takes the line and fill properties of the front object. Combining is reversible, but the component objects keep the line and fill properties of the combined object.

Combining is a quick way to create a mask or stencil cutout:

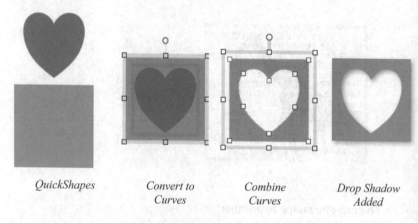

QuickShapes	*Convert to Curves*	*Combine Curves*	*Drop Shadow Added*

To combine two or more selected lines or drawn shapes:

1. Draw your two lines or QuickShapes.

2. Place the "clipping" object in front of the object to be cut out.

3. Select each object and choose **Tools>Convert To>Curves** for both.

4. Select both objects.

5. Choose **Combine Curves** from the **Arrange** menu.

To restore the original shapes from a combined object:

- Select it and choose **Split Curves** from the **Arrange** menu.

Adding anchors to objects

Anchors can be added to objects to allow hyperlinks and cross-references to link directly to a specific location rather than to the whole page. This is especially useful if you're referring to a page object such as an image or table, or to selected artistic or frame text.

Named anchors can optionally be included as PDF bookmarks. The anchor's name is added automatically to the PDF bookmark list as a new bookmark title; after generating your PDF, the bookmark can be clicked to navigate to that anchor location.

To add an anchor:

1. Select the object or portion of text.

2. Select **Anchor...** from the **Insert** menu.

3. From the dialog, enter a name for the anchor.

4. (Optional) Check **Include in PDF Bookmarks** if you want to create a PDF file which will show a bookmark which directs to the anchor's location. If checked, enter the **Bookmark title** that will show in the generated PDF.

5. Click **OK**.

Once created, you can insert hyperlinks, cross-references, and PDF bookmarks, directly linked to the new anchor.

To delete an anchor:

1. Select the object which has an anchor that you wish to remove.

2. Click **Anchor...** from the **Insert** menu (or **Insert Anchor...** from the right-click menu).

3. In the dialog, click **Delete**.

4. From the next dialog, you can either leave or delete all bookmarks or hyperlinks to the anchor independently of each other. Click Yes or No as appropriate.

Anchoring objects to text

If you're working with text frames you'll probably want to add supporting shapes, pictures, tables, or even nested text frames within your publication's text (artistic or frame text). Such objects can be positioned either in relation to a position in your text (or other page element) or be simply placed inline in your text. In either instance, objects can then move with the text as you add further text content.

In PagePlus, this positioning is controlled by **anchoring** an object using different positioning options.

- **Float with text**. The object is positioned relative to an ⚓ **anchor point** (horizontally and vertically). This option is ideal for pictures, pulled quotes, etc.

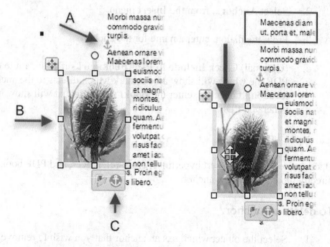

(A) Anchor point,
(B) Anchored object,
(C) Anchor properties

Pasted text causes reflow

- **Position inline as character**. The anchored object is placed as a character in the text and aligned in relation to the text that surrounds it. The anchored object flows with the text as before.

- **Detach from text**. The anchored object is disconnected from its anchor point, leaving a normal unanchored object.

PagePlus objects can be anchored to anywhere in your publication text, but the floated object can be positioned in relation to indented text, column, frame, page margin guides, the page itself, or most typically the anchor point in a text frame.

For text frames, when the text reflows, the anchor point (and therefore anchored object) reflows with the text. This allows supporting anchored objects to always stay with supporting text as more text is added to the frame.

To create an anchored object:

1. Position your unanchored object on the page.

2. Select **Anchor Object...** from the **Arrange** menu.

3. From the dialog, choose a positioning option:

Either, for a **floating** object:

1. Enable **Float with text**. This is the default positioning option.

2. Specify a **Horizontal** (e.g., Inside, Left-Aligned) and/or **Vertical position** (e.g., Inside, Top) in relation to different page elements, e.g. character (anchor point), frame, column, etc.

3. (Optional) Set an **Offset X by** or **Offset Y by** to further offset the object horizontally or vertically from the Horizontal and Vertical position in absolute units (centimetres or inches). Alternatively, check **Relative** to offset by a percentage of the object size. Check **Mirror facing pages** if you're using facing pages and you want the object to automatically mirror its position in relation to anchoring text moved onto a new page.

4. Check **Keep within bounds** to stop the anchored object from being placed outside of the text frame. The object will move but only to the frame edge or page margin guides. When unchecked there is no restriction on object placement.

5. (Optional) For control of possible object overlap, select an option from the **If objects overlaps** drop-down list.

   - **Allow the overlap**. The overlap is left as is.

   - **Pack into lines** means the second object will be placed beside the first object if there is room, or below it if not.

   - **Line up left to right/Line up right to left** means the second object will be placed to the right or the left of the first object, respectively.

   - **Stack top to bottom/Stack bottom to top** means the second object will be placed below or above the first object, respectively.

6. Click **OK**. The ⚓ **Anchor point** appears and your object is now an anchored (showing an ⚓ icon).

Or, for an **inline** object:

1. Enable **Position inline as character**.

2. To set the object's vertical alignment with respect to adjacent text, select an **Align with text** option. Text will not flow around the anchored object.

3. (Optional) Enter a **Offset Y by** value to set the percentage to which the object will be vertically offset in relation to its height.

4. (Optional) Check **Scale to** to scale the object to a percentage of the adjacent text point size. This keeps the same relative size if the text size changes. 100% will scale precisely to current point size.

5. (Optional) Check **Use these settings when pasting** to update floating and inline anchor defaults. Any subsequent object pasting will adopt the anchor settings saved when the option was checked.

6. Click **OK**. The object appears inline with text; an ⚓ **Anchor Properties** icon appears.

Objects inserted into text frames will automatically be anchored using "Float with text" default settings. However, the anchored object can be dragged away from the anchor point as an alternative method for creating an anchored object.

To view anchor properties:

1. Select an anchored object.

2. Click ⚓ **Anchor Properties** shown under the object.

The **Anchored Object Properties** dialog is displayed. The options differ depending on which of the three positioning options is enabled.

To change the position of an anchor point you can drag it anywhere else in your text frame. Dragging to an area of no text will disconnect your anchored object. You can also disconnect the anchor point via Anchor Properties dialog.

To disconnect an anchored object:

- Enable **Detach from text**. The Anchor Properties button and anchor point both disappear.

✎ Anchored object have all the same properties of unanchored objects; you can modify them whilst anchored.

✎ Frame text can wrap around floating anchored objects (see p. 139). Inline anchored objects don't allow text wrapping.

Joining object outlines

PagePlus includes some powerful tools to carve new shapes out of old overlapping shapes. With add, subtract, intersect, or exclude commands you actually produce a permanent new object (with a new outline) out of any selected objects. The joined object can be further edited by adjusting nodes in the new shape.

To join outlines:

1. Select objects.

2. Select an outlines option from the  **Join Outlines** flyout on the Arrange toolbar.

Add	Creates one new object that's the sum of any two selected objects.

The objects need not be overlapping.

Subtract	Discards the overlap between the top and bottom object. The top object is also discarded. Useful as a quick way of truncating shapes and pictures with another object.

Ensure the objects are overlapping!

Intersect   Retains the overlap and discards the rest.

Exclude   Merges two or more objects into a composite object, with a clear transparent "hole" where their filled regions overlap.

Applying a mesh warp envelope

Mesh warping lets you apply a preset warp envelope to your PagePlus object or bitmap (below), then optionally modify a flexible grid of points and lines that you can drag to deform or distort an object and (optionally) its fill.

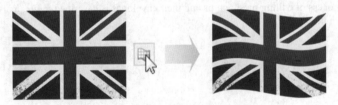

To apply a basic mesh warp to a selected object:

1. Click the down arrow on the 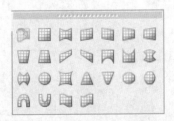 **Warp** flyout on the **Attributes** toolbar and choose a preset warp envelope from the displayed flyout.

The object deforms accordingly and a simple mesh outline appears around the object, with a node at each corner or around its outline.

2. You can use the Mesh Warp context toolbar to:

    •   **Disable Warp** temporarily.

    •   Choose a different **Preset Warp**.

    •   Specify with **Warp Fills** whether or not the warp effect extends to the object's gradient or bitmap fill or the bitmap's pixels.

Once created, selecting an existing envelope will activate the Pointer Tool (for manipulating the object), When you click on a node, the context toolbar lets you modify the selected node.

To enable a warp after disabling:

•   From the ▾ **Warp** flyout (**Attributes** toolbar), select **Reattach Warp** from the menu.

The process of editing mesh warps and their envelopes is described in greater detail in the PagePlus Help.

Adding borders

A **border** is a repeating, decorative element that can be set to enclose objects, such as text frames, pictures, and tables.

Lorem Ipsum
Curabitur felis erat, tempus eu, placerat et, pellentesque sed, purus. Sed sed diam. Nam nunc. Class aptent taciti sociosqu ad litora torquent per conubia nostra, per inceptos hymenaeos.

PagePlus comes with an impressive range of categorized picture-based border styles for you to use. However, if you'd like to create your own **custom** borders you can import a border design as a picture, and save it for future use.

Edge selection lets you apply the border effect to all sides, top, bottom, left, right, or both top and bottom (opposite).

 The Picture Frames category in the Gallery tab offers the same set of border styles but already applied to placeholder picture frames. (See p. 217.)

To add a border to an object:

1. Click ![Line/Border icon] **Line/Border** on the **Tools** toolbar's Fill flyout.

2. To define the border, select the **Border** tab, then select a border preset from the **Style** drop-down list. You can preview each border in the window at the right as you scroll down the open list with your keyboard up/down arrows.

To remove a border, select **None** from the top of the list.

3. Select a border **Weight** (width) for your border. You may need to experiment to find a width that complements the size of your object.

4. To apply the border to specific edges of the object, use the **Edge** drop-down menu.

☐ ▾
☐	Left Edge
☐	Top Edge
☐	Right Edge
☐	Bottom Edge
☐	No Edges
☐	Top and Bottom Edges
☐	All Edges

You can switch edges on and off to make multiple combinations.

5. Set other options as needed:

- Select a border **Type**. **Tile** repeats the edge design, Stretch simply stretches the design; **Single** scales the original picture to fit the object. Each preset's Type is already set so you may only need to adjust this for your own custom borders.

- Select an **Alignment** setting to fit the border to the **Outside**, **Inside**, or **Middle** of the object's bounding box.

- If **Behind contents** is checked, the inner half of the border extends behind the object. If unchecked, the whole border appears in front (the wider the border, the more it encroaches on the filled region).

- If **Scale with object** is checked, both border and object change together when you resize the object. If unchecked, the border weight remains constant during resizing.

- If **Draw centre** is unchecked (the default), the inside areas of a framed picture (used to create your new border) will be left empty, so you won't need to manually remove unwanted image centres. When checked, the area inside a populated custom frame is repeated.

6. Click **OK** when you're done.

Use the **Import...** button to base your borders on your own bordered picture design.

Once you've optimized the design of your new border, you might like to save it for future use. The border is stored globally so you can make use of it in other publications.

To save your custom border:

1. Click **Save as...**.

2. From the dialog, select a subcategory (e.g. Fun, Fabric, etc.) from the drop-down list; alternatively, enter a new custom subcategory name in the box. Click **OK**.

3. From the dialog, enter your custom border name and click **OK**. The new border appears in the Line and Border dialog's **Style** drop-down list (and also as a categorized bordered picture frame in the Gallery tab).

Adding logos

Logos are intended to send a clear message to your target audience, all within a simple and identifiable design. Whether you intend to communicate a stylish, business, fun or modern message (opposite), PagePlus allows you to create impressive logos of varying design.

Logos are great for adding to master pages associated with either publications (Paper Publishing mode) or websites (Web Publishing mode).

To add a logo:

1. Select ![icon] **Insert Logo** from the **Tools** toolbar's Logo flyout.

2. From the dialog, scroll the left-hand pane and select a suitable design thumbnail; choose the blank layout in the Blank category to start from scratch.

3. Select a logo from the left-hand pane, then pick from a choice of designs from the right-hand pane (if a choice is available); some designs allow customization of text.

4. To apply the publication's current colour scheme to your design, uncheck **Apply colour set**. Alternatively, to adopt a colour set independent of your publication's current colour scheme, keep **Apply colour set** checked and pick a colour set option from the drop-down list.

5. Click **Open**.

6. For captioned logos, a further dialog lets you customize the design's supporting text (company name and/or motto). Enter a new **Name** (e.g., company or club name) and, optionally, a tag line (**Motto**) to personalize it. Edit the text and then click **OK**.

7. To insert the logo at a default size, simply click the mouse to leave a logo placeholder (envelope).
   - or -
   To set the size of the logo, drag out a region and release the mouse button.

> PagePlus's Gallery tab also hosts the same selection of logos.

If you're looking to further modify your logo you can use **LogoStudio**, an integrated design environment. This allows you to focus on your design without the distractions of other objects on the page, i.e. the design is displayed in isolation and centred on the page. Alternatively, a logo or flash can be created from existing artistic text, shape, gallery object, picture, or grouped objects.

To edit an existing logo:

1. Click the  button on the control bar under the selected logo. LogoStudio is launched with your object(s) zoomed in to fit your workspace.

2. Using standard PagePlus tools and tabs, customize your logo design.

3. Click **✕ Close LogoStudio** from LogoStudio's main toolbar to exit. The modified logo is updated in its original position.

Converting objects to logos

It's just as easy to by-pass the pre-defined logos and base your custom logo on objects already present in your publication or website. The logo can be converted back to separate objects at any time by ungrouping.

To convert existing objects to a logo:

1. Select one or more objects (or a grouped object) on the page.

2. Select **Edit in LogoStudio...** from the **Edit** menu (or select via right-click).

3. Edit your logo design. In particular, you can use the upper **Logo Text** input box to "caption" your logo (typically a company or club name), then click the tick box.

Adding flashes

In PagePlus, **flashes** can be created, with each design intended to catch the eye, especially for commercial reasons or general attention grabbing.

PagePlus's Gallery tab comes complete with a host of flashes; subcategories based on Retail, Celebrations, Fun stuff (Shapes or Text), and Pointers are available.

When dragging a flash design onto the page, three varieties of flash may be encountered—those without text, with text, and those with optional layouts.

To add a flash:

1. From the **Gallery** tab, select the **Flashes** category.

2. Scroll the lower pane to preview flash subcategories; collapse unwanted subcategories by clicking the ⊟ button next to the subcategory name (click ⊞ to expand). Select a suitable flash thumbnail from the pane.

3. Drag your chosen design to the page.

4. From the dialog, you can choose design variations, edit text and apply colours, i.e.

- **For design variations**. Select a design from the **Designs** pane (e.g., offering different text labels and positions).

- **For text**. If the selected design has supporting text, you can customize it in the **Text** or **Message** field. Edit the text accordingly to give your flash meaning.

- **For colour**: To apply the publication's current colour scheme to your design, uncheck **Apply colour set**. Alternatively, keep **Apply colour set** checked and pick a colour set option from the drop-down list.

5. Click **OK**.

If you're looking to further customize your flash design (or use existing page objects) you can use **LogoStudio**. See Adding logos on p. 93.

5 Working with Text

Importing text from a file

Importing text from a word-processor file is the traditional way to create text content for Desktop Publishing layouts (but you can also create a story using WritePlus). If you use your current word processor to create the text file for your publication, you can import any number of files into one publication. Each file becomes a **story** consisting of a self-contained section of text like a single article in a newspaper, which resides in one or more linked **text frames**.

As well as the WritePlus format (.stt), a range of popular word processing and text formats can be imported, including:

ANSI text	.txt
Microsoft Word 2007/2010	.docx/.dotx
Microsoft Word 2000/2003	.doc/.dot
MS Works	.wps
Open Office text	.odt
Rich Text Format	.rtf
Wordperfect	.wpd
Write	.wri

For Microsoft Word formats created in any Windows operating system you don't need to have Microsoft Word installed locally. This means you can reuse third-party text content in PagePlus without the supporting application.

> PagePlus will preserve the formatting of imported word-processor text. However, if you're using your word processor to create text specifically for PagePlus, you'll save time by typing as text only, and applying formatting later in PagePlus.

To import text from a file:

1. (Optional) If using an existing empty text frame, select the frame. If inserting text into a populated text frame, click for an insertion point (or select a portion of text to be replaced).

2. Choose **Text File...** from the **Insert** menu.

3. From the **Open** dialog, locate and select the file to import.

4. Check the **Retain Format** box to retain the source file's formatting styles. Uncheck the box to discard this information. In either case, PagePlus will preserve basic character properties like italic, bold, and underline, and paragraph properties like alignment (left, centre, right).

5. Check the **Ignore line wrapping** box to ignore returns in the source text—that is, only if the file has been saved with a carriage return at the end of every line, and you want to strip off these extra returns. Otherwise, leave the box unchecked.

6. Click **Open**.

7. The text will be imported into the pre-selected text object or a new text frame. If all of the imported text cannot fit into the active text frame you'll be prompted via dialog. You can either create extra frames to accommodate overflow text (click **Yes**) or just overflow the text into a hidden overflow area (click **No**).

Understanding text frames

Typically, text in PagePlus goes into **text frames**, which work equally well as containers for single words, standalone paragraphs, or multipage articles or chapter text. You can also use **artistic text** (see p. 112) for standalone text with special effects, or **table text** (on p. 157) for row-and-column displays.

What's a text frame?

A text frame is effectively a mini-page, with:

*   Margins and column guides to control text flow.

*   Optional preceding and following frames.

*   Text and optional inline images that flow through the frames.

The text in a frame is called a **story**.

*   When you move a text frame, its story text moves with it.

*   When you resize a text frame, its story text reflows to the new dimensions.

Frames can be linked so that a single story continues from one frame to another. But text frames can just as easily stand alone. Thus in any publication, you can create text in a single frame, spread a story over several frames, and/or include many independent frame sequences. By placing text frames anywhere, in any order, you can build up newspaper or newsletter style publications with a story flowing from one column to another (below) or even across pages.

Frame 1   *Frame 2*

Mauris purus. Donec est nunc, ornare non, aliquet non, tempus vel, dolor. Integer sapien nibh, egestas ut, cursus sit amet, faucibus a, sapien. Vestibulum purus purus, elementum ac, luctus ullamcorper, ornare vitae, massa. Nullam posuere sem ut mauris. Nullam velit. Quisque sodales. Donec suscipit suscipit erat. Nam blandit. Praesent congue lorem non dolor. Maecenas vitae erat. Ut ac purus vel purus dapibus gravida.

Nullam lorem sapien, tempus ac, fringilla at, elementum sed, purus. Duis molestie pede. Vivamus quis odio sit amet libero sodales tincidunt. Nam sit amet metus vitae lectus ullamcorper dignissim. Suspendisse leo. Praesent turpis justo, Mauris purus. Donec est nunc, ornare non, aliquet non, tempus

vel, dolor. Integer sapien nibh, egestas ut, cursus sit amet, faucibus a, sapien. Vestibulum purus purus, elementum ac, luctus ullamcorper, ornare vitae, massa. Nullam posuere sem ut mauris. Nullam velit. Quisque sodales. Donec suscipit suscipit erat. Nam blandit. Praesent congue lorem non dolor. Maecenas vitae erat. Ut ac purus vel purus dapibus gravida.

Nullam lorem sapien, tempus ac, fringilla at, elementum sed, purus. Duis molestie pede. Vivamus quis odio sit amet libero sodales

Text frames have a range of properties and operations that can be performed on them. Here's a breakdown of text frame capabilities.

Feature	Supported
Margins and column guides	✓
Breaks (column, page, and frame)	✓
Resize/move frame	✓
Crop frame	✓
Rotate frame	✓[1]
Frame linking	✓

Columns	✓
Export as text	✓
Line attributes	✓
Solid fill and line colour	✓
Gradient and bitmap fill	✓
Transparency	✓[1]
Borders	✓[1]
Warp	✓[1]
2D/3D Filter Effects	✓[1]
Instant 3D	✓[1]

[1] If applied, will export frame as a graphic (Web Publishing mode only).

Creating text frames

You add frames to a page as you would any other object. PagePlus supports a wide variety of frame shapes which can be resized and morphed into new shapes once placed on the page (just like QuickShapes; see p. 201).

To create a frame:

1. Select a standard or shaped text frame from the ▣ ▾ **Text Frame** flyout on the **Tools** toolbar.

2. Click on the page or pasteboard to create a new frame at a default size.
   - or -
   Drag out to place the text frame at your chosen dimensions.

To create a frame (from a shape):

- You can also draw a shape and select **Convert to>Shaped Text Frame** on the **Tools** menu (text is not auto-aligned).
  - or -

- For QuickShapes, type directly onto the QuickShape to automatically create a shaped frame (text is automatically centred vertically and horizontally). Useful for creating objects for diagrams!

To delete a frame:

- Select the frame—click its edge until a solid border appears—and then press the **Delete** key.

You can select, move, and resize text frames just like other objects. (See p. 63, 72, and 72, respectively.) When you select a frame's bounding box, indicated by a solid border line plus corner and edge handles, you can manage the frame properties; selecting inside a frame created a blinking insertion point in the frame's text (the frame's boundary box becomes hatched to indicate editing mode). In this mode, you can edit the text. (For details, see Editing text on the page on p. 117.)

Putting text into a frame

You can put text into a frame using one of the following methods:

WritePlus story editor:	With a selected frame, click ▣ **WritePlus** on the Frame context toolbar.
Importing text:	Right-click on a frame and choose **Insert Text File...** (shortcut **Ctrl+T**) to import text.
Typing into the frame:	Select the Pointer Tool, then click for an insertion point to type text straight into a frame, or edit existing text.
Pasting via the Clipboard:	At an insertion point in the text, press **Ctrl+V**.
Drag and drop:	Select text (e.g. in a word processor file), then drag it onto the PagePlus page. If you drop onto a selected frame, the text is pasted inline where the insertion point had been placed previously. Otherwise, a new frame is created for the text.

Frame setup and layout

The **frame layout** controls how text will flow in the frame. The frame can contain multiple **columns**. When a frame is selected, its column margins appear as dashed grey guide lines if set in **Frame Setup**. Note that unlike the page margin and row/column guides, which serve as layout guides for placing page elements, the frame column guides actually determine how text flows within each frame. Text won't flow outside the column margins.

You can drag the column guides or use a dialog to adjust the top and bottom **column blinds** and the left and right **column margins**.

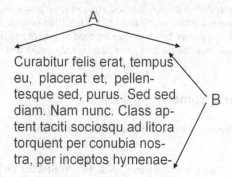

Curabitur felis erat, tempus eu, placerat et, pellentesque sed, purus. Sed sed diam. Nam nunc. Class aptent taciti sociosqu ad litora torquent per conubia nostra, per inceptos hymenae-

A - Column margins, B - Column blinds

To edit frame properties directly:

- Select the frame object, then drag column guide lines to adjust the boundaries of the column.

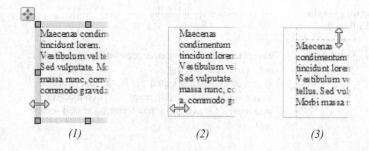

(1)   *(2)*   *(3)*

The illustration above shows how the cursor will change when hovering over the **selected** bounding box (1), after dragging inwards the column margin can be adjusted (2), and after dragging downwards, the top margin blind can be moved (3).

To edit frame properties using a dialog:

1. Select the frame and click ![icon] **Frame Setup** on the Frame context toolbar.

2. From the dialog, you can change the **Number of columns**, **Gutter** distance between columns, **Left Margin**, **Right Margin**, and enable/disable text wrapping around an object.

3. To change the column widths and blinds (top and bottom frame margins), click a cell in the table and enter a new value.

How a story flows through a sequence of frames

You can have just one frame on its own, or you can have many frames. Frames can be connected in linked **sequences** so that the **story** associated with a given frame sequence flows through the first frame on to the next and keeps flowing into frames in the link sequence.

A key difference from a word processor is that PagePlus does not normally add or remove frames according to the amount of text. The text simply flows until the text runs out (and some frames are left empty), or the frames run out (and some text is left over), i.e.

- If the text runs out before the last frame, you have some empty frames. These frames will be filled with text if you add more text to the story, or if you increase the size of the story text.

- If there is still more text to go after filling the last frame, PagePlus stores it in an invisible **overflow area**, remembering that it's part of the story text. If you later add more frames or reduce the size of text in a frame, the rest of the story text is flowed in.

PagePlus keeps track of multiple linked frame sequences, and lets you flow several stories in the same publication. The **Text Manager** (accessed via the **Tools** menu) provides an overview of all stories and lets you choose which one you want to edit.

On text overflow, the frame's ⊞ AutoFlow button can be used to create new frames for the overflowed text. To control how the frame text is spread throughout available frames, you can use **Fit Text**, **Enlarge Text**, or **Shrink Text**. These options scale a story's text size.

Fitting text to frames

Fitting story text precisely into a sequence of frames is part of the art of laying out publications.

If there's too much story text to fit in a frame sequence, PagePlus stores it in an invisible **overflow area** and the Link button on the last frame of the sequence displays ■ ; an ⊞ **AutoFlow** button appears next to the Link button. You might edit the story down or make more room for it by adding an extra frame or two to the sequence. Clicking the AutoFlow button adds additional frames and pages as needed (see below).

Once frames are in position it's still possible to control how text is distributed throughout the frame(s) via tools on the Frame context toolbar.

Ⓐ ▾   The **Text Sizing** flyout offers three tools for controlling how frame text scales through the text frame. These are "once-off" operations (compared to the "continuous" **Autofit** options shown below).

Ⓐ   **Fit Text**
Click to scale the story's text size so it fits exactly into the available frame(s); further text added to the frame will cause text overflow. You can use this early on, to gauge how the story fits, or near the end, to apply the finishing touch. Fit Text first applies small point size changes, then small leading changes, then adjustments to the paragraph space below value, until the text fits.

Ⓐ   **Enlarge Text**
Click to increase the story's text size one increment (approx. 2%).

Ⓐ   **Shrink Text**
Click to reduce the story's text size one increment.

Each frame's story text can adopt its own individual autofit setting as follows:

 The **AutoFit Options** flyout offers three autofit options which continuously act upon a selected frame's story text.

 No Autofit
This is the normal mode of operation where, if selected, text won't automatically scale throughout the selected text frame, possibly leaving partly empty frames at the end of the frame sequence.

 Shrink Text on Overflow
If selected, extra text added to a selected frame will shrink all frame text to avoid text overflow.

 Autofit
If selected, the frame will always scale text automatically by adjusting text size (compare to **Fit Text** which fits text once, with any additional text causing text overflow).

AutoFlow

When importing text, it's a good idea to take advantage of the **AutoFlow** feature, which will automatically create text frames and pages until all the text has been imported. This way, enough frames are created to display the whole story. Then you can gauge just how much adjustment will be needed to fit the story to the available "real estate" in your publication.

If you add more text to a story while editing, or have reduced the size of frame, you may find that an overflow condition crops up. In this case you can decide whether to use AutoFit or click the frame's **AutoFlow** button.

To AutoFlow story text on the page:

- Click the ⊞ **AutoFlow** button just to the left of the frame's ▣ **Link** button.

If no other empty frames are detected, you'll be prompted to autoflow text into a new frame(s) the same size as the original or to new frame(s) sized to the page. If an empty frame exists anywhere in your publication, PagePlus will flow text into that instead, before commencing with autoflow.

Linking text frames

When a text frame is selected, the frame includes a **Link** button at the bottom right which denotes the state of the frame and its story text, and which allows you to control how the frame's story flows to following frames:

▣ **No Overflow**
The frame is not linked to a following frame (it's either a standalone frame or the last frame in a sequence) and the frame is empty or the end of the story text is visible.

▣ **Overflow**
The populated frame is not linked (either standalone or last frame) and there is additional story text in the **hidden** overflow area. An ⊞ **Autoflow** button also appears to the left of the **Link** button.

▽ **Continued**
The frame is linked to a following frame. The end of the story text may be visible, or it may flow into the following frame.
Note: The button icon will be red if the final frame of the sequence is overflowing, or green if there's no overflow.

There are two basic ways to set up a linked sequence of frames:

- You can link a sequence of empty frames, then import the text.

- You can import the text into a single frame, then create and link additional frames into which the text automatically flows.

> When frames are created by the AutoFlow option (for example when importing text), they are automatically linked in sequence.

To create a link or reorder the links between existing frames, you can use the **Link** button under the frame (or the controls on the Frame context toolbar). Remember to watch the cursor, which changes to indicate these operations.

- You can link to frames already containing text or are already in a link sequence.

- If the frame was not part of a link sequence, its text is merged into the selected text's story.

- Different frame sequences can be combined, creating unified story text.

To link the selected frame to an existing frame:

- Click the frame's **Link** button (showing or .)

- Click with the Textflow cursor on the frame to be linked to.

To link the selected frame to a newly drawn frame:

- As above, but instead of clicking a "target" frame, either click on the page (for a default frame) or drag across the page (to create a frame sized to your requirements). The latter is ideal for quickly mapping out linked frames across different pages.

To unlink the selected frame from the sequence:

- Click , then click with the Textflow cursor on the same frame.

Story text remains with the "old" frames. For example, if you detach the second frame of a three-frame sequence, the story text remains in the first and third frames, which are now linked into a two-frame story. The detached frame is always empty.

To navigate from frame to frame:

- Click in the text at the end of a text frame, then use your down arrow keyboard key to jump to the next frame.

Using artistic text

Artistic text is standalone text you type directly onto a page. Especially useful for headlines, pull quotes, and other special-purpose text, it's easily formatted with the standard text tools.

Here are some similarities between frame text and artistic text. Both text types let you:

- vary character and paragraph properties, apply named text styles, edit text in WritePlus and even import text.

- apply different line styles, fills (including gradient and bitmap fills), and transparency.

- access text via the Text Manager.

- track font usage with the Resource Manager.

- embed inline images.

- apply 2D/3D filter effects and rotate/flip.

- use proofing options such as AutoSpell/Spell Checker, Proof Reader, and Thesaurus.

And some differences...

- You can initially "draw" artistic text at a desired point size, and drag it to adjust the size later. Frame text reflows in its frame upon frame resize (but doesn't alter its text size).

- Artistic text can be applied to a path but frame text cannot.

- Artistic text won't automatically line wrap like frame text.

- Artistic text doesn't flow or link the way frame text does; the Frame context toolbar's text-fitting functions aren't applicable to artistic text.

To create artistic text:

1. Choose the **A** **Artistic Text Tool** from the **A ▾** **Artistic Text** flyout on the **Tools** toolbar.

2. Set initial text properties (font, style, etc.) as needed before typing, using the Text context toolbar, **Format** menu, or right-click (and choose **Text Format**>).

3. Click on the page for an insertion point using a default point size, or drag the cross-hair cursor across the page to specify a particular size, e.g.

4. Type directly on the page to create the artistic text.

Once you've created an artistic text object, you can select, move, resize, delete, and copy it just as you would with a text frame. Solid colours, gradient/bitmap fills, and transparency can all be applied.

To resize or reproportion an artistic text object:

- To resize while maintaining the object's proportions, drag the resize handles.

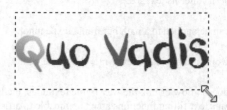

- To resize freely, hold down the **Shift** key while dragging.

To edit artistic text:

- Drag to select a range of text, creating a blue selection.

You can also double-click to select a word, or triple-click to select all text.

Now you can type new text, apply character and paragraph formatting, edit the text in WritePlus, apply proofing options, and so on.

Putting text on a path

"Ordinary" straight-line artistic text is far from ordinary—but you can extend its creative possibilities even further by flowing it along a curved path.

The resulting object has all the properties of artistic text, plus its path is a Bézier curve that you can edit with the Pointer Tool as easily as any other line! In addition, text on a path is editable in some unique ways, as described below.

To apply a preset curved path to text:

1. Create an artistic text object.

2. With the text selected, on the Text context toolbar, click the ✗ ▾ **Path Text** flyout and choose a preset path.

The text now flows along the specified path, e.g. for "Path - Top Circle".

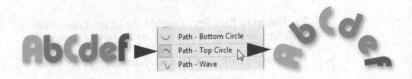

To add artistic text along an existing line or shape:

1. Create a freehand, straight, or curved line (see Drawing and editing lines on p. 196) or a shape (see Drawing and editing shapes on p. 201).

2. Choose the **A** **Artistic Text Tool** from the **A** ▾ **Artistic Text** flyout on the **Tools** toolbar.

3. Bring the cursor very close to the line. When the cursor changes to include a curve, click the mouse where you want the text to begin.

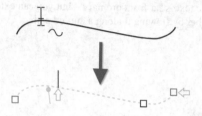

4. Begin typing at the insertion point. Text flows along the line, which has been converted to a path.

To fit existing text to an existing line or shape:

1. Create an artistic text object.

2. Create a freehand, straight, or curved line or a shape.

3. Select both objects. On the **Tools** menu, choose **Fit Text to Curve**. The text now flows along the specified path.

To create text and path at the same time:

1. Choose one of the Path Text tools from the  **Artistic Text** flyout on the **Tools** toolbar:

   The **Freehand Path Text Tool** lets you sketch a curved line in a freeform way.

   The **Straight Path Text Tool** is for drawing a straight line.

   The **Curved Path Text Tool** lets you join a series of line segments (which may be curved or straight) using "connect the dots" mouse clicks.

2. Create a line on the page. Your line appears as a path with an insertion point at its starting end (for a curved path, press **Esc** or double-click).

3. Begin typing at the insertion point. Text flows along the path.

To remove the text path:

1. Select the path text object.

2. Click ✗ **Path - None** on the Text context toolbar's Path flyout.

The text remains as a straight-line artistic text object and the path is permanently removed.

Editing text on the page

You can use the Pointer Tool to edit frame text, table text, or artistic text directly. On the page, you can select and enter text, set paragraph indents and tab stops, change text properties, apply text styles, and use Find and Replace. For editing longer stories, and for more advanced options, choose WritePlus (**Edit Story...** from the **Edit** menu).

Selecting and entering text

The selection of frame text, artistic text, and table text follows the conventions of the most up-to-date word-processing tools. The selection area is shaded in semi-transparent blue for clear editing.

> Nulla vestibulum eleifend
> nulla. Suspendisse potenti.
> Aliquam turpis nisi, venenatis
> non, accumsan nec, imperdiet
> laoreet, lacus.

Double-, triple- or quadruple-click selects a word, paragraph or all text, respectively. You can also make use of the **Ctrl**-click or drag for selection of non-adjacent words, the **Shift** key for ranges of text.

To edit text on the page:

1. Select the Pointer Tool, then click (or drag) in the text object. A standard insertion point appears at the click position (see below),
    - or -
    Select a single word, paragraph or portion of text.

2. Type to insert new text or overwrite selected text, respectively.

Nulla |vestibulum eleifend
nulla. Suspendisse potenti.
Aliquam turpis nisi, venenatis
non, accumsan nec, imperdiet
laoreet, lacus.

To start a new paragraph:

- Press **Enter**.

To start a new line within the same paragraph (using a "line break" or "soft return"):

- Press **Shift+Enter**.

The following two options apply only to frame text. You can use these shortcuts or choose the items from the **Insert>Break** submenu.

To flow text to the next column (Column Break), frame (Frame Break) or page (Page Break):

- Press **Ctrl+Enter**, **Alt+Enter** or **Ctrl+Shift+Enter**, respectively.

To switch between insert mode and overwrite mode:

- Press the **Insert** key.

To show special characters:

- Click the **¶ ▾** drop-down arrow on the **View** toolbar, either for **Show Special Characters** (paragraph marks and breaks; see below) or **Show Spaces** (Show Special Characters plus tabs, non-breaking spaces, hyphenation points, and "filled" normal spaces).

Praesent nisl tortor, laoreet eu,
dapibus quis, egestas non,
mauris.
 Cum sociis natoque penatibus,
nascetur ridiculus mus.

Nullam eleifend pharetra felis.
Mauris nibh velit, tristique
lacinia in.

Praesent nisl tortor, laoreet eu,
dapibus quis, egestas non,
mauris.↵
 Cum sociis natoque penatibus,
nascetur ridiculus mus.¶

Nullam eleifend pharetra felis.
Mauris nibh velit, tristique
lacinia in.§

Copying, pasting, and moving text

You can easily copy and paste text using standard commands; drag and drop of
text is also supported.

> ✎ If you don't place an insertion point on pasting, the text can be
> pasted into a new text frame directly.

Setting paragraph indents

When a text object is selected, markers on the horizontal ruler indicate the left
indent, first line indent, and right indent of the current paragraph. You can adjust
the markers to set paragraph indents, or use a dialog.

- The **Left** indent (**A**) is set in relation to the object's left margin.

- The **1st line** indent (**B**) is in relation to the left indent.

- The **Right** indent (**C**) is in relation to the object's right margin.

For details on setting frame margins, see Frame setup and layout (on p. 106).

To set the indents of the current paragraph:

- Drag the appropriate ruler marker(s) as shown above.
  - or -

- For quick left indents, select the **Increase Level** or
  Decrease Level button to increase or decrease indent, respectively.
  Indent is by the currently set default tab stop distance.
  - or -

- To adjust indent settings numerically, choose **Paragraph...** from the
  Format menu. In the Indentation box, you can enter values for Left,
  Right, 1st Line, or Hanging indents.

Setting tab stops

To set a tab stop:

1. Select the paragraph(s) in which you want to set tab stops.

2. Click the ruler intersection button until it changes to the type of tab
   you want: (Left, Centre, Right, or Decimal).

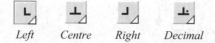

Left *Centre* *Right* *Decimal*

3. Click on the horizontal ruler where you want to set a tab stop. You'll
   see your tab stop appear.

   - To move a tab stop, drag it to a new ruler position.

   - To delete a tab stop, drag it off the ruler.

If you want to set precise measurements for tabs, right-click the
frame and choose **Text Format**, then select **Tabs...** from the
submenu.

Working with Unicode text

PagePlus fully supports Unicode, making it possible to incorporate foreign characters or special symbols.

- To paste Unicode text from the Clipboard to the page, use **Edit>Paste Special...**, then select "Unformatted Unicode Text."

- Insert Unicode characters directly into your text by typing your Unicode Hex value and pressing **Alt+X**. The Alt+X keyboard operation toggles between the displayed character (e.g., @) and its Hex value (e.g., U+0040) equivalent.

- To export text in Unicode format, use WritePlus.

Using Find and Replace

You can search publication text for an extraordinary variety of items: not just words or parts of words, but a host of character and paragraph attributes such as fonts, styles, alignment, bullets and numbering, missing fonts, drop caps... even inline graphics and more! Once located, you can replace items either globally, or on a case-by-case basis.

To use Find and Replace on frame text:

1. Choose **Find & Replace...** from the **Edit** menu.

2. In the dialog, type the text to be found in the **Find** box and its replacement text (if any) in the **Replace** box. Click the down arrows to view recent items. Click either box's button to use flyout menus to select formats or special characters, or define a regular expression (for a wildcard-type search).

3. Select the Range to be searched: **Current Story** (just the currently selected text object or story), or **All Stories** (all text), or **Current Selection** (only used with the Replace All function to operate on the currently selected text).

4. Select **Match whole word only** to match character sequences that have **white space** (space, tab character, page break, etc.) or punctuation at each end, or which are at the start/end of a paragraph. Select **Match case** for case-sensitive search. Select **Regular expressions** to treat the contents of the Find box as an expression, rather than as a literal string to be found.

5. Click **Find Next** to locate the first instance of the Find text.
   - or -
   Click **Select All** to highlight all instances of matching text in your document simultaneously.

6. Click **Replace** if you want to substitute with replacement text. Alternatively, click **Find Next** again to skip to the next matching text. Continue using the Replace option as required until you reach the end of your document.
   - or -
   Click **Replace All** to replace all instances of the found text with the replacement text at the same time. PagePlus reports when the search is completed.

7. Click **Close** to dismiss the Find and Replace dialog.

Setting text properties

PagePlus gives you a high degree of typographic control over characters and paragraphs, whether you're working with frame text, table text, or artistic text.

To apply basic text formatting:

1. Select the text.

2. Use buttons on the Text context toolbar to change text style, font, point size, attributes, paragraph alignment, bullets/numbering, or level.

To clear local formatting (restore plain/default text properties):

- Select a range of text with local formatting.

- Click on the **Clear Formatting** option on the Text context toolbar's text styles drop-down list (or Text Styles tab).

Using fonts

One of the most dramatic ways to change your document's appearance is to change the fonts used in your artistic text, frame text, or table text. Applying different fonts to a character or entire paragraph can communicate very different messages to your intended readership.

Lorem Ipsum

LOREM IPSUM

Lorem Ipsum

Lorem Ipsum

Lorem Ipsum

Font assignment is very simple in PagePlus, and can be done from the **Fonts tab**, Text context toolbar, or in the **Character** dialog (via right-click, or from the **Format** menu).

A font belongs to one of the following types as indicated by the symbol before the font's name.

T	TrueType
O	OpenType
A	Type 1 (PostScript)
畐	Raster (bitmap)

The Fonts tab lets you:

- Apply fonts easily without dialog navigation.

- Assign fonts to be Websafe or favourites.

- View most recently used, Websafe, and your favourite fonts simultaneously.

- Search for installed fonts via search box.

- Hover-over preview of fonts applied to your document's text (optional).

- Change a font for another throughout your publication or website (by right-click Select All).

- Access Serif FontManager (if purchased).

The Fonts tab is automatically hidden by default, but can be viewed by clicking the arrow button at the left of your workspace. You may also need to click the **Fonts** label to display the **Fonts** tab.

Assigning and previewing fonts

The fonts shown in the **Fonts** tab represent the currently installed fonts on your computer. This means that these fonts are available to format any selected character or paragraph.

To assign a font:

- Select some text, then click on the font name in the Fonts tab to assign the font to the text.

You can preview how fonts will appear on your selected text by enabling PagePlus's font preview feature.

To preview fonts:

1. From the tab's ▷ **Tab Menu** button (top-right of tab), check the **Preview Font** option.

2. Select a section of text (a letter, word, or paragraph) in your document.

3. On the **Fonts** tab, hover over any font in the list. The selected text will update to show how the font will appear in situ.

4. (Optional) Click on the font in the Fonts tab to assign the font to the text.

Changing common fonts

Changing one font for another is very simple for a single portion of text, but the **Fonts** tab can take things a step further by allowing a font to be located throughout the entire document (see above), and if necessary, swapped for another font. It's simple to then re-assign a different font to the selected text.

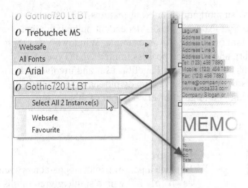

To select (and change) a font throughout your document:

1. Right-click a font displayed in the **Fonts** tab.

   If the font is used in your document, you'll see a "*Select All n Instance(s)*" message (*n* is the number of times the font is used). If there are no occurrences, you'll get a "*Not currently used*" message.

2. Click the message label, making it shaded in blue—text formatted with the chosen font is selected.

3. Hover over font names in your font list. Click on a chosen font to apply it to the selected text (if you've used the Used fonts search you may need to clear the results before selecting a replacement font).

Fonts with OpenType features

Microsoft Windows supplies OpenType and TrueType font types as standard.

You'll be able to spot these font types by their symbols (O and T for OpenType and TrueType, respectively) shown in your Font drop-down list on the Text context toolbar, in the Text Style dialog, and in the fonts list in the Fonts tab.

To extend the capability of your installed font, PagePlus allows you to take advantage of additional **font features** built into your font's design. These allow font characters to be changed either via substitution rules or by manual choice. As an example you may see extra **glyphs**, i.e. letter shape variations, appear on the character.

Note that some fonts don't support additional font features, with others supporting only a limited font features. This is dependent on how the font designer has created the font originally. As an example, Windows Vista fonts such as Constantia, Calibri, and Cambria possess limited OpenType font features. However, if you're a professional PagePlus user and involved with advanced typography, it's likely that you've already purchased and installed professional fonts, allowing you to get the very best out of this feature.

Font-dependent features may include:

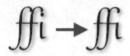

Ligatures
Replace a pair or triplet of characters such as "fi" of "ffi" with a single glyph. In this case it avoids the problem of the dot of the "i" conflicting visually with the hook of the "f". Discretionary ligatures are not used as standard because they are typically too ornate for standard text/ They are more decorative and, as the name implies, are intended to be substituted manually.

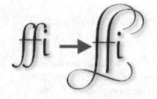

Stylistic Sets/Stylistic Alternates
Stylistic sets can give you many options of what you want the font to look like and combine preset choices such as which ligatures and alternates are available by default. These can be especially ornate or flowing versions of a glyph (sometimes called "swash" variants). This may be as simple as offering a "g" with and without a closed loop.

$Abc \rightarrow Abc$

Small Caps/Petite Caps
A small cap "A" should use a special glyph, which typically looks like a capital "A", but is shorter, but has the same stem widths etc. as the capital, so it can't be achieved by just scaling the capital. Petite caps are like small caps but even smaller.

$(CAPS) \rightarrow (CAPS)$

Case sensitive forms
These are variants of punctuation such as brackets that, for example, are designed to align more nicely with capitals. These would generally sit a little higher in the line, because most capitals don't have descenders.

$12^{th} \rightarrow 12^{th}$

Superscripts and subscripts
These are smaller raised or lowered versions of characters; the scaling issues are the same as for Small Caps. Some fonts also provide **Ordinals**, which are a form of superscript intended to be used for the letters in "2nd", or forms that are intended to be used in chemical or mathematical notation.

$1/3 \rightarrow \frac{1}{3}$

Fractions
In text like "1/3", the digits before the slash are made smaller and raised, and the digits after the slash are made smaller and may be lowered. A special narrow version of the slash may be used.

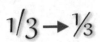

Old style figures
These are digits that have a bit more character (at right); they often sit lower in the line. Compare with the more usual "lining" figures that are more uniform (at left).

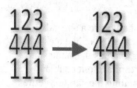

Proportional figures

These are variable width digits (at right); for example, a "1" that is narrower than a "2", which would look good when set in body text, as opposed to the more usual tabular figures (at left) that are all the same width so they line up in columns or tables.

As for any other text attribute, you can apply the font feature to selected characters or to a text style equally either from the Text context toolbar or Text Style dialog, respectively. The option names are similar in both locations. Options vary according to font. If no options are offered, the font does not provide any additional font features.

To apply OpenType features to selected characters:

1. Select your text which has the OpenType font assigned to it.

2. From the Text context toolbar, click the down arrow on the **OpenType flyout**. On the flyout, the displayed options (showing sample text and hover preview) vary according to the features supported by the OpenType font.

3. Select an option(s) from the flyout.

To apply OpenType features to text styles:

1. From **Format>Character**, select the **Character - OpenType** option.
   Expand the tree for all OpenType features.

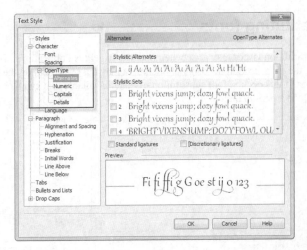

2. Enable font features under the Alternates, Numeric, Capitals, and
   Details sections.

   - **Alternates**: The OpenType Alternates dialog (above) offers
     glyph substitutions or alternate representations such as swashes,
     stylistic sets, contextual alternates, stylistic alternates, and titling
     alternates.

   - **Numeric**: offers OpenType features used primarily when setting
     numbers, e.g. Figure Styles, Figure Width, and Number Position.

   - **Capitals**: groups case-base features together such as small caps,
     petite caps, and case-sensitive forms.

   - **Details**: dynamically displays every OpenType feature in list
     form, derived from the font's internal tables. As such you can set
     less common OpenType Features, unavailable from the previous
     Alternates, Numeric, and Capitals sections.

If an option is shown in brackets it is not supported by the currently used font. This allows the feature to be switched on for text styles, where the current font isn't known.

Substituting fonts

Font substitution issues may arise when opening PagePlus Publications. This is because the fonts used in the original document may not be present on the target computer. If this occurs, font substitution of that unavailable font can be initiated via a pop-up dialog.

PagePlus's font substitution mechanism makes use of the PANOSE Font Matching System which intelligently finds the best font substitution match between a missing and a locally available font. By default, clicking **OK** will substitute the missing font for a locally available standard font (e.g., Arial) automatically. Optionally, you can manually substitute the missing font with the font of your choosing by enabling the **Edit font substitutions manually** button instead.

A third option, is to use Serif's FontManager program which can search and load uninstalled fonts if located (fonts are uninstalled after use).

 To avoid font substitution, try to source original fonts from the originating PC if possible.

When importing PDF files, PagePlus attempts to reuse embedded fonts and perform font substitution.

To manually substitute a font on loading a publication:

1. Enable the **Edit font substitutions manually** button on the initial dialog, and click **OK**.

2. From the Resource Manager, click the **Fonts** tab, and select the font with status "Missing". Click **Substitutions**.

3. From the **Substitute Missing Fonts** dialog, choose a replacement font from the **Available fonts** list box ensuring that the **Bold** and/or **Italic** options are checked if necessary. Some fonts may be a more acceptable substitute with the bold or italic style set.

4. Click **Add<<** to place the font in the **Substitute with** box. This box can contain more than one font—your first choice and a secondary font (e.g., Arial or Times New Roman). A secondary font (perhaps a more widely available font) is particularly useful if you want to provide an alternative to your first choice substituted font. You should always place your first choice at the top of the list with the **Move up** or **Move down** buttons. The dialog shows both fonts for substitutions.

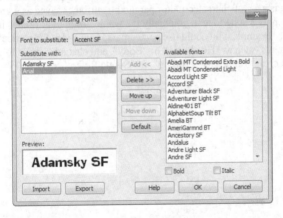

The Adamsky SF font is first choice, with Arial used as a secondary font.

5. Click **OK**.

Reset the **Substitute with** box by clicking the **Default** button. This will replace the fonts listed with a single font, e.g. Arial or Times New Roman, as governed by Windows (this is not configurable).

To manually substitute a font any time:

1. Select **Resource Manager** from the **Tools** menu.

2. Choose the **Fonts** tab, select a font from the list, and click the **Substitutions** button.

3. In the dialog, select the missing font to be substituted from the **Font to substitute** drop-down menu.

4. Carry out font substitution as described in the previous procedure. Repeat for each font to be substituted using the **Font to substitute** drop-down menu.

Using text styles

PagePlus lets you use named **text styles** (pre- or user-defined), which can be applied to frame text, table text, artistic text, index text or table of contents text. A text style is a set of character and/or paragraph attributes saved as a group. When you apply a style to text, you apply the whole group of attributes in just one step. For example, you could use named paragraph styles for particular layout elements, such as "Heading 1" or "Body", and character styles to convey meaning, such as "Emphasis", "Strong", or "Subtle Reference".

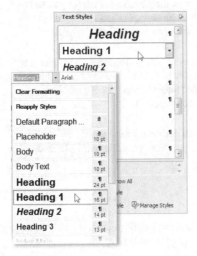

Styles can be applied to characters or paragraphs using either the Text context toolbar or the Text Styles tab. Both paragraph and character styles can be managed from the **Text Style Palette**.

Paragraph and character styles

A **paragraph style** is a complete specification for the appearance of a paragraph, including all font and paragraph format attributes. Every paragraph in PagePlus has a paragraph style associated with it.

- PagePlus includes a built-in **default** paragraph style called **"Normal"** which is left-aligned, 12pt Times New Roman. When you create frame text from scratch you'll be using the **Body** text style based on Normal; artistic text uses **Artistic Body** text style, based on the Body style. This hierarchical approach makes for powerful text style control.

- Applying a paragraph style to text updates all the text in the paragraph except sections that have been locally formatted. For example, a single word marked as bold would remain bold when the paragraph style was updated or changed.

A **character style** includes only font attributes (name, point size, bold, italic, etc.), and you apply it at the character level—that is, to a range of selected characters—rather than to the whole paragraph.

- Typically, a character style applies emphasis (such as italics, bolding or colour) to whatever underlying font the text already uses; the assumption is that you want to keep that underlying font the same.

The base character style is shown in the Text Styles tab (or palette) as **"Default Paragraph Font**," which has no specified attributes but basically means "whatever font the paragraph style already uses."

- Applying the Default Paragraph Font option from the Text Styles tab (or the Text context toolbar's Styles box) will strip any selected local character formatting you've added and will restores original text attributes (paragraph styles are not affected).

- As with paragraph styles, you can define any number of new character styles using different names and attributes (or adopt a pre-defined character style).

Text style hierarchies

All paragraph or character text styles available in PagePlus are ultimately based on the respective Normal and Default Paragraph Font text styles.

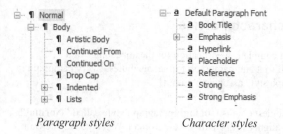

Paragraph styles   *Character styles*

So why have this hierarchy of text styles? The key reason for this is the ability to change a text style at any "level" in the hierarchy in order to affect all "child" styles which belong to it.

Working with named styles

Normal ▾ The named style of the currently selected text is displayed in either the Text Styles tab or the **Styles** drop-down list on the Text context toolbar. A character style (if one is applied locally) may be shown; otherwise it indicates the paragraph style.

To apply a named style:

1. Using the Pointer Tool, click in a paragraph (if applying a paragraph style) or select a range of text (if applying a character style).

2. Display the **Text Styles** tab and select a style from the style list.
   - or -
   On the Text context toolbar, click the arrow to expand the Styles drop-down list and select a style name.

The Text Style tab highlights the paragraph or character style applied to any selected text.

As both paragraph and character formatting can be applied to the same text, all of the current text's formatting is displayed in the **Current format** box on the tab. In the example below, currently selected text has a Strong character style applied over a Normal paragraph style.

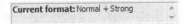

To update a named style using the properties of existing text:

1. Make your desired formatting changes to any text that uses a named style.

2. On the **Text Styles** tab, right-click the style and choose **Update <style> to Match Selection**.

All text using the named style, throughout the publication, takes on the new properties.

To create a new paragraph or character style:

1. Either:

   1. On the **Text Styles** tab, select the paragraph or character style on which you want your new style to be based.

   2. Click the ⬚+ **Create Paragraph Style** or ⬚+ **Create Character Style**.

   - or -

- Choose **Text Style Palette...** in the **Format** menu, and with a "base" style selected in the dialog, click the **Create...** button.

2. In the **Text Style** dialog, define the style **Name**, the style to be **Based on**, **Style for the following paragraph**, and the style to be changed to if **Increase Level** is applied. Check **Always list in Studio** to ensure the style will always appear in the **Text Styles** tab.

3. In the left tree menu change any character or paragraph attributes, tabs, bullets, and drop caps you want to include in the new style definition.

4. Click **OK** to create the style, or **Cancel** to abandon changes.

To create a new style using the properties of existing text:

1. Format the text as desired.

2. To define a character style, select a range of reformatted text. To define a paragraph style, deselect text but leave a blinking cursor (insertion point) within the newly formatted section.

3. Type a new style name into the Text context toolbar's **Styles** drop-down list and press **Enter**.

The new style is defined with the properties of the selected text.

To modify an existing style:

1. From the Text Styles tab:

   - Right-click on the character or paragraph style you want to modify and then choose **Modify <style>...**
     - or -

   - With a style selected, pick the 🄰 **Manage Styles** button from the **Text Styles** tab, then choose the **Modify...** button.

2. From the Text Style dialog, define (or change) the style name, base style, and any character or paragraph attributes, tabs, bullets, and drop caps you want to include in the style definition.

3. Click **OK** to accept style properties, or **Cancel** to abandon changes.

4. Click **Apply** to update text, or click **Close** to maintain the style in the publication for future use.

Alternatively, choose **Text Style Palette...** from the **Format** menu to modify styles and to change text defaults (see p. 29).

To delete one or more text styles:

- Right-click a text style and select **Delete <style>...**.

- From the dialog, click **Remove**. For deletion of multiple styles, check multiple style names first. For removal of all or unused styles, use appropriate buttons.

> ◌ Take care when deleting styles. Styles based on a checked "parent" style will be checked for deletion.

Removing local formatting

To return characters and/or paragraphs back to their original formatting, click on the **Clear Formatting** option in the Text Styles tab. This is great for reverting some formatting which hasn't quite worked out! You can clear the formatting of selected characters, paragraphs, or both depending on what text is currently selected. The following table indicates the effects of different types of text selection on clear formatting.

Selection	Clicking Clear Formatting affects..
Word	Character
Range of text	Character
Single paragraph	Character and Paragraph
Multiple paragraphs	Paragraph
Story text	Character and Paragraph
Text frame	Character and Paragraph

You also have the flexibility to be more explicit about how clear formatting is applied by clicking on the Clear Formatting option's drop-down arrow, i.e.

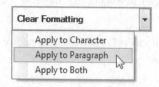

To remove local formatting:

1. Select locally formatted characters or paragraph(s) as described in the above table.

2. Either:

   - Select **Clear Formatting** from the **Styles** drop-down list on the Text context toolbar.
     - or -

   - On the **Text Styles** tab, click the **Clear Formatting** option.
     - or -
     From the same tab, select **Apply to Both** from the drop-down menu or **Clear Text Formatting** from the **Format** menu).
     - or -
     Select **Apply to Character** to remove all local character formatting (leaving paragraph formatting untouched).
     - or -
     Select **Apply to Paragraph** to remove all local paragraph formatting (leaving character formatting untouched).

Like **Clear Formatting**, you can use **Reapply Styles** on the **Text Styles** tab (or Text context toolbar) to clear all local overrides leaving the default text. However, where Clear Formatting reverts the text to Normal style, Reapply styles reverts the text back to its current name style. Use **Apply to Character** (retaining paragraph styles overrides), **Apply to Paragraph** (retaining character style overrides), and **Apply to Both** to remove both character or paragraph style overrides simultaneously.

If you prefer, you can remove a style's formatting, enabling you to start building up your text style again. Choose **Manage Styles** button on the Text Styles tab, click the **Modify** button, then click the **Clear All** button from the General section.

Changing common styles

Changing one character or paragraph style for another is very simple for a single portion of text. However, in PagePlus, it's just as easy to swap one style for another by selecting multiple instances of the style and choosing an alternative style. This swaps styles across paragraphs and throughout entire stories all at the same time.

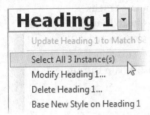

To select (and change) a style throughout your document:

1. Right-click a style displayed on the **Text Styles** tab.

2. If the style is used in your document, you'll see a "*Select All n instance(s)*" message (*n* is the number of times the style is used).

    If there are no occurrences of the style, you'll see a "*Not currently used*" message.

3. Click the message label—text formatted with the chosen style is highlighted.

4. Hover over style names in your styles list, then click on a chosen style to apply the style to the selected text.

Wrapping text

PagePlus lets you wrap frame text around the contours of a separate object. Usually, this means wrapping text to a picture that overlaps or sits above a text frame. But you can wrap frame text around a picture, shape, artistic text, table, or another frame. Wrapping is accomplished by changing the **wrap setting** for the object to which text will wrap.

Vestibulum semper enim non eros. Sed vitae arcu.
Aliquam erat volutpat. Praesent odio nisl, suscipit
at, rhoncus sit amet,
porttitor sit amet, leo.
Aenean hendrerit est.
Etiam ac augue. Morbi
tincidunt neque ut lacus.
Duis vulputate cursus
orci. Mauris justo lorem,
scelerisque sit amet, placerat sed,
condimentum in, leo. Donec urna est, semper
quis, auctor eget, ultrices in, purus. Etiam rutrum.

To wrap text around an object:

1. Select the object around which you want the text to wrap.

2. Click the 🖳 **Wrap Settings** button on the **Arrange** toolbar..

3. Select the manner in which text will wrap around the object by
   clicking a sample, i.e.

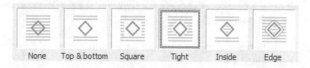

4. Choose which side(s) the chosen wrapping method will be applied,
   again by clicking a sample.

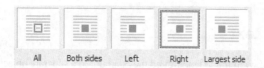

The examples show tight wrapping applies to the right of the object
only.

5. Click **OK**.

In addition, you can specify the **Distance from text**: the "standoff" between the object's **wrap outline** and adjacent text. (The wrap outline is a contour that defines the object's edges for text wrapping purposes.) Different object types have different initial wrap outlines. For QuickShapes, the wrap outline corresponds exactly to the object's edges, while for closed shapes the outline is a rectangle.

You can manually adjust the wrap outline using the Curve context toolbar for more precise text fitting. See PagePlus help for more information.

Creating a bulleted or numbered list

You can turn a series of paragraphs into **bulleted**, **numbered** or **multi-level lists**. Bullets are especially useful when listing items of interest in no specific order of preference, numbered lists for presenting step-by-step procedures (by number or letter), and multi-level lists for more intelligent hierarchical lists with prefixed numbers, symbols, or a mix of both, all with supporting optional text (see Using multi-level lists on p. 143).

Bulleted list   *Numbered list*   *Multi-level list*

PagePlus lets you create simple lists directly from the Text context toolbar or choose from a preset bullet, number or multi-level lists via dialog. If you want to go a step further you can create custom list styles by selecting your own symbols, numbers and letter formats. You then have the option of replacing an existing preset with your own preset based on your own custom list style.

Lists can be applied to normal text (as local formatting) or to text styles equally.

To create a simple bulleted or numbered list:

1. Select one or more paragraphs.
   - or -
   Click in a paragraph's text.

2. Select ☷ **Bulleted List** or ☶ **Numbered List** from the Text context toolbar.

The list style used is the first preset shown in the Bullets & Numbering dialog described below.

To create a bulleted or numbered list (using presets):

1. Select one or more paragraphs.
   - or -
   Click in a paragraph's text.

2. Select **Bullets and Numbering...** from the **Format** menu.

3. From the Text Style dialog's Bullets and Numbering menu option, choose **Bullet**, **Number**, or **Multi-Level** from the **Style** drop-down menu.

4. Select one of the preset formats shown by default.
   - or -
   For a custom list, click the **Details** button to display, then alter custom options.

5. Click **OK** to apply list formatting.

💡 For number and multi-level lists, check **Restart numbering** to restart numbering from the current cursor position in the list; otherwise, leave the option unchecked.

💡 Turn off list formatting by clicking the ☷ or ☶ buttons on the Text context toolbar again.

Using multi-level lists

1. Vestibulum velit orci.
   Nullam sed enim. Du
   1.1 Lorem ipsum
       pendisse poter
   1.2 Mauris vitae a
       nean arcu elit.
       ligula.
       1.2.1 Quisqu
       1.2.2 Donec
             Duis b
             molest
             tum le
2. In hac habitasse plate
   Proin mattis eleifend
3. Proin mattis eleifend
   pede tellus, dictum eg

For multi-level lists, as opposed to bulleted and numbered lists, you can set a different character (symbol, text or number) to display at each level of your list. Levels are normally considered to be subordinate to each other, where Level 1 (first level), Level 2 (second), Level 3 (third), etc. are of decreasing importance in the list. For example, the following simple multi-level numbered passage of text is arranged at three levels.

The flexibility of PagePlus's multi-level bullet and numbering system means that you have full control over what gets displayed at each level. For this reason, no common numbering schema needs to exist between levels, i.e. the list could equally be prefixed with a different symbol, text prefix, or number combination at each level.

If you apply a multi-level preset to a range of text you'll get a list with the preset's Level 1 format applied by default. Unless you use text styles, you'll have to change to levels 2, 3, 4, etc. to set the correct level for your list entry.

Changing list levels on selected paragraphs:

- Click the ![Increase Level icon] **Increase Level** or ![Decrease Level icon] **Decrease Level** button on the Text context toolbar to increment or decrement the current level by one.

The multi-level presets offer some simple but commonly used schemas for paragraph list formatting. However, if you want to create your own lists or modify an existing list (your own or a preset), use the **Details** button in the Text Style dialog when Multi-Level style is selected. See PagePlus Help for more details.

Assigning bullets, numbers, and levels to styles

The lists discussed so far are usually applied as local formatting to a single style, typically "Normal" or "Body". To prove this, you'll see the list structure disappear if you apply **Clear Formatting** (from the Text Styles tab or Text context toolbar's Styles drop-down menu) on the selected list.

If you're working on long documents, you may be using pre-assigned text styles (Heading 1, Heading 2, indent, etc.) to format your document rather than using the above local formatting. You can use such text styles along with list styles to number headings or paragraphs automatically without the need to repetitively format headings or paragraphs as lists. As an example, headings and paragraphs in technical and legal documents are typically prefixed by numbers for easy reference. The advantage of using a style-driven approach is that you can let the numbering take care of itself while you concentrate on applying styling to your document.

If you plan to create your own multi-level paragraph styles, make use of the **Style for Increase Level** option when creating text styles. This sets the paragraph style that will be automatically applied to text if **Increase Level** is applied from the context toolbar; another advantage is that if you apply a multi-level style to text, the associated next level's style will be made available in the Text Styles tab.

PagePlus lets you easily associate any bulleted, numbered or multi-level list style (either preset or custom list) to an existing text style. See Using text styles on p. 132.

Inserting cross-references

PagePlus allows you to cross-reference to headings and anchored text, tables, pictures, or diagrams throughout your publication. Numbered paragraphs, footnotes/endnotes, and next/previous frames can also be cross-referenced.

By choosing the "target" of the cross-reference, i.e. what the reference is to (e.g., a heading or anchor), you can then choose how the cross-reference will appear, typically as a page number or item name. This can also appear as the text "above" or "below", a text number, or referenced header/content.

To insert a cross-reference field:

1. (Optional) In advance, create anchors to any objects you'd like to cross-reference to.

2. Click in the text for an insertion point (or make a text selection).

3. Choose **Information** from the **Insert** menu, then select **Cross-reference...** from the submenu.

4. From the dialog, choose a target that you want to reference to from the **Type** drop-down list. Types include:

    -   **Anchor**: a named anchor, which may be attached to an object or text via **Insert>Anchor...**.

- **Bookmark**: a named bookmark as assigned with **Insert>PDF Bookmarks...**.

- **Heading**: a paragraph of text formatted with a heading text style (e.g. Heading 1).

- **Numbered paragraph**: text formatted as a numbered list or numbered heading.

- **Footnote or endnote**: the first paragraph of a footnote or an endnote.

- **Next frame/Previous frame**: when text flows through a series of linked frames you can reference the subsequent text frame into which the current frame's text will next flow. Previous does the reverse—you reference the previous text frame from which the flowing text has comes from.

4. In the **Item** list, which changes with the Type selected, select the item of that type in your publication. These can be sorted alphabetically or by page number, by clicking on the appropriate column.

5. The **Insert as** section lets you choose how the reference will appear. You can pick from one of several choices of target.

- **Page number**: the number of the page the target is on.

- **Above/below**: the position of the target relative to the cross-reference. This may also display as "left" or "right" if the target is on the same page, or "opposite" in a publication with facing pages.

- **Item name**: For anchors and bookmarks only, the name is taken from the target's Name shown in the previous Item list.

- The remaining options only make sense when the target is text:

  - **Text number**: the number of the numbered list, heading, footnote or paragraph. When the target is deep in a multi-level numbered list, like "1.B.iii.", you can pick:

    - (no context): just the target's own number, e.g. "iii.".

- (relative context): which list levels are included depends on whether the cross-reference is in part of the same list as the target. For example, if the cross-reference is in "1.C.ii." (a later part of the same top-level list), then the reference would appear as "B.iii".

- (full context): include numbers from all levels of the list, e.g. "1.B.iii.".

For a normal paragraph (not in a numbered list or footnote), its number is the count from its most recent heading, and the full context includes the text of that heading. For example, "Details/3" would refer to the 3rd paragraph since the "Details" heading.

- **Referenced header**: the text of the most recent header of the target. Use this for referencing heading text.

- **Referenced content**: the actual text of the target paragraph. You can limit the number of words to be included with the **Up to** input box; set this to a large number to get the entire paragraph.

6. **Prefix/Suffix**: Use to add text before and after the reference. For example, you could surround a reference with brackets or quotes, or include "p. " as a prefix to a page number reference.

7. **Number separator**. Often numbered lists include their own separators and punctuation, for example "(A)". This check box discards the original separator and replaces it with the given new one, entered into the adjacent box. This is especially useful with multi-level lists with context, where "1.(A)1." can be reformatted by the cross-reference as, for example, "1.A.1".

8. Keep **Insert as Hyperlink** checked to make the cross-reference a hyperlink; this is ideal for electronic publishing to PDF or when exporting to HTML (in web publishing mode). For printing to desktop printers, uncheck the option if needed.

9. Click **OK**.

To edit a cross-reference:

- Right-click the cross-reference field and select **Edit Cross-reference**.

To jump to a cross-referenced target:

- Right-click the cross-reference field and select **Go To Target**.

Continued From/Continued On cross-references

For easy story navigation between linked text frames, PagePlus provides **"Continued From/Continued On"** cross-references. When enabled, these appear at the top and bottom of your text frame, respectively, to indicate where the story text continues, i.e. to the previous or next text frame on the same or different publication page.

viverra malesuada, enim
. Cras risus turpis, varius
onummy felis. Etiam
cipit erat, nec suscipit sem

(Continued on __page 2__)

Like other cross-references, these references will automatically update if frames are moved to a different page or new pages are added.

To insert a "Continued From/On" cross-reference:

1. Select the text frame which is linked to another frame you want to reference to.

2. Choose **Information** from the **Insert** menu, then select **Continued From** or **Continued On** from the submenu. The cross-reference appears at the top or bottom of the text frame, respectively.

By default, you'll create a page number cross-reference. However you can change the cross-reference to a different Type by right-clicking the field and selecting **Edit Cross-reference**.

Inserting user details

When you create a publication from a design template for the first time, you may be prompted to update your user details (Name, Company, Telephone number, etc.) in a User Details dialog. These details will automatically populate pre-defined text "fields" in your publication, making it personalized.

You can also use this User Details dialog to review and update user details at any time, as well as define global and publication variables for use in all PagePlus publications or just the current publication.

To add, edit or change User Details:

1. Click the  **Set User Details** button on the Pages context toolbar (deselect objects to view).

2. Enter new information into the spaces on the **Business** or **Home** tab (a **Calendars** tab will appear if there is a calendar in your publication).

You can also insert one or more User Details fields into any publication at any time.

To insert a User Detail field:

1. Select the Pointer Tool and click in the text for an insertion point.

2. Choose **Information** from the **Insert** menu, then select **User Details...** from the submenu.

3. Select a User Detail entry, and optionally any text **Prefix** or **Suffix** to include with your user details, e.g. *Name:*.

4. Click **OK**.

For existing publication, the fields (once edited) can be updated at the click of a button.

To update fields:

- Enter new information in the User Details dialog (via **Tools>Set User Details...**).

- Click the **Update** button to automatically update any altered field currently placed in your publication. This field will remain linked to User Details until it is deleted.

Inserting variables

If you have some repeating text used throughout your publication which you'd like to swap for replacement text, you can use **variables**. Typically, you would do this to change a product name or version, making your publication easy to update when product versions change. The variable fields change automatically, updating with the new values.

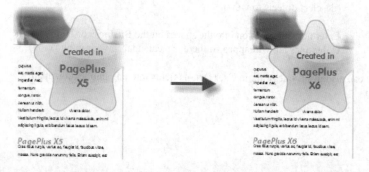

Variables are used in a similar way to user details (see p. 149). They can be added and inserted just like user detail fields and be updated from the same User Details dialog.

The variable can be stored just within the publication or made globally for other publications. The latter would be a good choice for product names as they are likely to be used again globally in a company environment.

To add, edit or delete variables:

1. Click  **Set User Details** on the Pages context toolbar.

2. Select the **Global** or **Publication** tab if you want the added variable to be available to all publications or just to the document, respectively.

3. From either tab, click the **Add** button.

4. In the variables list, type over the created **Variable** name, giving it a unique string that identifies the variable easily.

Variable	Value
Product_Name_Version	

5. Click in the column adjacent to the new Variable and type the variable value (i.e. the text that will appear on the page).

Variable	Value
Product_Name_Version	PagePlus X5

6. Add additional variables as required to either the Publication or Global tab.

7. Click **Update**.

Once you've decided on your choice of variables you can insert variables as fields in place of "static" text. You can't take advantage of variables unless they are inserted into your publication.

To insert a variable field:

1. Click in the text for an insertion point (or make a text selection).

2. Choose **Information** from the **Insert** menu, then select **Variable...** from the submenu.

3. Select a variable entry, and optionally any text **Prefix** or **Suffix** to include with your variable.

4. Click **OK**.

When you want to change the variable, all that's needed is to edit and update the variable's value. The variable fields throughout your publication are updated with the new values.

To update variables:

1. Click ⬚ **Set User Details** on the Pages context toolbar (deselect objects to view).

2. Edit the existing variables with new values.

Variable	Value
Product_Name_Version	PagePlus X6

3. Click **Update**.

Using Auto-Correct and Spell as you Type

PagePlus includes two powerful support tools to nip possible spelling errors in the bud. The **Auto-Correct** feature overcomes common typing errors and lets you build a custom list of letter combinations and substitutions to be applied automatically as you type. You can also **underline spelling mistakes as you type** to mark possible problem words in your story text with red underline. Both features apply to frame text, table text, and artistic text.

If you prefer to address spelling issues in larger doses at the same time, you can run the Spell Checker anytime.

Auto-Correct

To set options for automatic text correction:

1. Choose **Options...** from the **Tools** menu and select the **Text>Auto-Correct>Options** page.

2. Check your desired Auto-Correct options as required.

For any checked options, auto-correction will be enabled. Additionally, a pre-defined correction list for automatic text replacement can be used; the list, populated by commonly typed misspellings and their correct equivalents, can also be added to for custom corrections.

To use a correction list:

1. Choose **Options...** from the **Tools** menu and select the **Text>Auto-Correct>Replacements** page.

2. Check **Replace text while typing** to turn on Auto-Correct. The pre-defined text replacements will be applied when you type the misspelt words.

To add custom misspellings to the correction list:

1. In the **Replace** field, type a name for the Auto-Correct entry. This is the abbreviation or word to be replaced automatically as you type. For example, if you frequently mistype "product" as "prodcut," type "prodcut" in the Replace box.

2. In the **With** field, type the text to be automatically inserted in place of the abbreviation or word in the **Replace** field.

3. Click the **Add** button to add the new entry to the list.

4. To modify an entry in the correction list, select it in the list, then edit it in the **Replace** and **With** field above. Click the **Replace** button below.

5. To remove an entry, select it and click **Delete**.

Spell as you Type

Use this feature to firstly indicate possible problem words in your text using red underline, and secondly to offer (via right-click) a range of alternative correct spellings to replace the problem words.

To check spelling as you type:

- Ensure the **Underline spelling mistakes as you type** feature is turned on (from **Tools>Options>Text>Proofreading**).

In your document, words with spelling problems are indicated with a red squiggly underline. You can review these by eye, with the option of replacing the words with suggested alternatives.

- To replace a marked word, place an insertion point in a marked word then right-click to choose an alternative spelling from the context menu.

- To tell PagePlus to ignore (leave unmarked) all instances of the marked word in the publication, choose **Ignore All** (or just **Ignore** for this instance only).

- To add the marked word (as spelled) to your personal dictionary, choose **Add to Dictionary** from the right-click menu. This means PagePlus will subsequently ignore the word in any publication.

- Select **Check Spelling** to run the Spell Checker described above.

Spell-checking

The **Spell Checker** lets you check the spelling of a text in your current story, all stories on the current page, or all stories in your publication. You can customize the built-in dictionary by adding your own words.

To help trap typographic errors and fix spelling problems while creating text, use Auto-Correct and Check spelling as you type, respectively.

Multilingual spell checking is supported by use of up to 14 dictionaries. Any language can be enabled globally from **Tools>Options>Text>Proofreading** or applied specifically to text or paragraphs via the Language Selector in the Character tab. Spell checking can be turned off temporarily by selecting "None" as a language type—this could be useful when working with text containing lots of unusual terms (perhaps scientific or proprietary terminology).

To check spelling:

1. (Optional) To check a single story, first make sure the text or text object is selected.

2. Choose **Spell Checker...** from the **Tools** menu.

3. (Optional) In the dialog, click **Options...** to set preferences for ignoring words in certain categories, such as words containing numbers or domain names.

4. Select **Check currently selected story only**, **Check all stories on the current page**, or **Check all stories in my publication** to select the scope of the search.

5. Click **Start** to begin the spelling check.

When a problem is found, PagePlus highlights the problem word. The dialog offers alternative suggestions, and you can choose to **Change** or **Ignore** this instance (or all instances) of the problem word, with the option of adding the problem word to your dictionary.

6. Spell checking continues until you click the **Close** button or the spell-check is completed.

Automatic proofreading

The **Proof Reader** checks for grammar and readability errors in text in your publication. You can use Proof Reader from either PagePlus or WritePlus.

To start automatic proofreading:

1. To check a single story, first make sure the text or text object is selected.

2. Choose **Proof Reader...** from the **Tools** menu.

3. If necessary, click the **Options** button to set options for proofreading, including a spell-check option and the level of formality (with checks for rule types).

4. Select options to **Check currently selected story only**, **Check all stories on the current page,** or **Check all stories in my publication** to select the scope of the search.

5. Click **Start** to begin proof reading.

When a problem is found, PagePlus highlights the problem word. The dialog offers alternative suggestions, and you can choose to **Change** or **Ignore** this instance (or all instances) of the problem word.

6. Proofreading continues until you click the **Close** button or the process is completed.

> ✦ You can use a **Thesaurus** to find synonyms, definitions, and variations of words in your publication text, via the **Tools** menu. See PagePlus Help for more details.

Creating text-based tables

Tables are ideal for presenting text and data in a variety of easily customizable row-and-column formats, with built-in spreadsheet capabilities.

			£/€
Ranunculus aquatilis	345-56	1	4.24/4.97
Myosotis scorpiodes	334-B299	2	4.64/5.44
Nympholdes peltata	089-78	2	2.93/3.44
Menyanthes trifoliate	455-01	1	7.10/8.32
Caltha palustris	345-33	1	2.55/2.99

Each cell in a table behaves like a mini-frame. Like frame text you can vary character and paragraph properties, apply named text styles, apply photo-based borders, embed inline images, apply text colour fills (solid, gradient, or bitmap), track font usage with the Resource Manager, and use proofing options such as Spell Checker, Proof Reader, and Thesaurus. Some unique features include number formatting and formula insertion.

Feature	Supported
Resize/move table	✓
Rotate table	✓[1]
Rotate table text (in cell)	✓[1]
Sort table contents	✓
Solid fill and border colour	✓
Gradient and bitmap fill	✓
Transparency	✓[1]
Borders	✓[1]
Warp	✓[1]

2D/3D Filter effects	✓[1]
Instant 3D	✓[1]
QuickClear/QuickFill/AutoFormat	✓
Edit cell text in WritePlus	✓
View cell text in Text Manager	✓
Pasting of Excel cell contents	✓

[1] If applied, will export table as a graphic (Web Publishing mode only).

> 🖎 Table text doesn't flow or link the way frame text does; the Frame context toolbar's text-fitting functions aren't applicable.

Rather than starting from scratch, PagePlus is supplied with a selection of pre-defined table formats, i.e. templates, that can be used. Simply pick one and fill in the cells with content.

PagePlus lets you:

- Edit the pre-defined format before adding a new table to the page.

- Create your own custom formats without creating a table. See Creating custom table formats in PagePlus Help.

- Edit existing tables to fit a different format (pre-defined or custom).

To create a table:

1. On the **Tools** toolbar, choose the ▦ **Table Tool** from the ▦ ▾ **Table** flyout.

2. Click on the page or pasteboard, or drag to set the table's dimensions. The **Create Table** dialog opens with a selection of preset table formats shown in the **Format** window.

3. Step through the list to preview the layouts and select one. To begin with a plain table, select **(Default)**.

4. (Optional) Click **Edit** if you want to further customize your chosen format.

5. Set the **Table Size**. This is the number of rows and columns that make up the table layout.

6. Click **OK**. The new table appears on the page.

> 💡 Plan your table layout in advance, considering the number of rows/columns needed!

Inserting a calendar

The **Calendar Wizard** helps you design month-at-a-glance calendars for use in your publication.

JANUARY 2011	
1	S
2	S
3	M
4	T
5	W
6	T
7	F

The calendar is created as a scalable text-based table so you can edit text using the standard text tools. The properties of a selected calendar are similar to those of a table, and can be modified identically. Like custom table formats you can create your own custom calendar formats.

The wizard lets you set up the month/year and calendar style/format, and controls the inclusion of personal events and/or public holidays. The **Calendar Event Manager** lets you add personal events before or after adding a calendar to the page.

For calendar-specific properties, a context toolbar lets you change an existing calendar's month/year, modify calendar-specific properties, and manage calendar events (both personal and public holidays).

At any time, you can update calendar details throughout your publication via **Set User Details**—in the same way that you'd set up the date (along with the time) on some alarm clocks. This is especially useful if you want to update the year on a year-to-view page, composed of 12 monthly calendars—you only need to change the year in one place.

> If you have adopted a calendar-based design template, you'll be initially prompted to configure global calendar details via a User Details dialog. This updates all calendar details throughout your PagePlus document.

To insert a calendar:

1. Click the Table flyout on the **Tools** toolbar and choose **Insert Calendar**.

2. Click again on your page, or drag out to set the desired size of the calendar.

3. From the displayed **Calendar Wizard**, define options for your calendar including setting the year and month, calendar style (square, or in single or double column format), week start day, room to write, display options, switching on personal events/holidays, and calendar format.

    To have your country's public holidays shown, check **Add public holidays** in the wizard and select a **Region** from the associated drop-down menu. To add personal events, check **Add personal events** additionally.

4. Click **Finish** to complete the wizard.

If you plan to use your calendar in subsequent years, simply update the **Year** setting in **Tools>Set User Details**.

To view and edit a selected calendar's properties:

1. Click 📅 **Edit Calendar** on the Calendar context toolbar.

2. Choose an appropriate tab and make your modification, then press **OK**.

Right-click on a row/column header within the calendar to select, insert, delete, and adjust widths/heights for rows (or columns), as well as autofit to cell contents, but take care not to corrupt your table formatting!

Adding public holidays

When you create a calendar you can set up the appropriate public holidays for the country you reside in. The holidays will show up in your calendar automatically if **Add public holidays** is checked in Calendar Properties.

To enable public holidays:

1. Select your calendar's bounding box, and click 📅 **Edit Calendar** on the context toolbar.

2. From the Events tab, check **Add public holidays**.

3. (Optional) Swap to a different country's public holiday settings by using the **Region** drop-down list.

4. Click **OK**.

To display public holidays:

1. Select your calendar's bounding box.

2. Click 🎈 **Calendar Events** on the context toolbar.

3. Enable the **Show public holidays** option.

Adding personal events

You can complement your public holiday listings (e.g., Easter holidays) by adding personal events such as birthdays, anniversaries, and bill payments (unfortunately!) so that the events show up on your calendar—simply use the **Calendar Events** button on a selected calendar's context toolbar. Events show automatically on your calendar under the chosen date.

To add an event:

1. Select your calendar's bounding box.

2. Click 🎈 **Calendar Events** on the context toolbar.

3. Ensure that the **Show personal events** option is selected.

4. (Optional) Select **Show events by date** to view your events in a more traditional calendar layout.

5. Click 📋 **New event**.

6. From the dialog, type, use the up/down arrows, or click the ⟨...⟩ **Browse** button to select a date.

7. Enter your event text into the text input box. This displays in your calendar under the chosen date.

8. If the event is a birthday or other annual event, check **Event recurs annually**.

9. Click **OK**. The event appears in the event list under the chosen date.

10. When you have finished adding events, click **Save**.

💡 Use the 📋 **Edit event** or ✕ **Delete event** buttons to modify or delete an existing event.

Inserting database tables

As a great way of producing a database report in your publication, it is possible for a database table to be imported and presented as a PagePlus table. The database table could be from one of a comprehensive range of database file formats (Serif databases (*.sdb), Microsoft Access, dBASE), as well as from HTML files, Excel files, ODBC, and various delimited text files.

For multi-table databases, PagePlus lets you select the table to be inserted.

For a high degree of control, it is also possible to filter and sort your database records prior to import.

> Insertion of database tables adopts the same principles as those used for Mail merge (see p. 172). However, instead of creating letters or labels you are merging content into a table.

To insert a database table:

1. Click 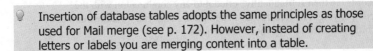 **Insert Database table** from the **Tools** toolbar's Table flyout.

2. Using the pointer, draw an area on your page that will contain your database information.

> If there are many fields in your database table you may consider presenting the information on a page with landscape orientation. Alternatively, you can choose only a subset of those fields (see below).

3. In the dialog, navigate to your database file and select it. Use the drop-down menu to change file format if you can't find the database file you require.

4. Click **Open**.

5. (Optional; for multi-table databases) The **Select Table** dialog displays the tables within your database. Select your table and click **OK**.

6. The **Merge List** dialog shows all the table rows (records) in the table—choose to **Select All** records, **Toggle Select** (invert all current selections) or use a custom **Filter...** The filter option also lets you sort

the records to be merged. The **Edit...** button lets you edit Serif Database SDB files only. Click **OK**.

7. The list of fields available in the table is shown in the **Select Fields** dialog. Uncheck any fields that you don't want to be included in the import process. Again, Select All, Select None, or Toggle Select options are available.

8. Click the **OK** button. The database table appears on your page.

Filtering your records

Records can be filtered via the Merge List's **Filter...** button by using the Filter Records tab then subsequently sorted into any combination with the accompanying Sort Records tab. The option helps you limit the number of records imported to only those you require.

You can use the Boolean operators "And" and "Or" to build up your filter criteria row-by-row.

The Sort Records tab is used to sort by three prioritized field names, either in ascending or descending order.

Creating a table of contents

The Table of Contents Wizard (**Insert>Table of Contents...**) helps you create a table of contents with up to six levels of headings and sub-headings derived from named styles in your publication.

If you're exporting to PDF format, PagePlus can automatically build a bookmark list using the same style markings in your text.

To create a table of contents:

1. Decide which named styles you want to designate as headings at each of up to six levels.

2. Check your publication to make sure these styles are used consistently.

3. Review the choices you'll need to make when you run the Table of Contents Wizard.

4. From the **Insert** menu, choose **Table of Contents...** to run the Wizard.

5. You can easily modify the look of your table of contents, or run the Wizard again to update the information.

You can optionally hyperlink each page number to its actual page location. (See Hyperlinking an object on p. 170.)

Using styles to prepare a table of contents

The Wizard will show you a list of all the style names used in your publication, and you will check boxes to include text of a given style as a heading at a particular level (1 through 6). For example, you could pull out all text using the "Heading" style as your first-level headings.

Entries in the resulting table of contents will appear in the order the text occurs in your publication.

When the table of contents is created, PagePlus formats it using built-in text styles (p. 132) intended specifically for table of contents preparation: "Contents-Title" and "Contents-1st" through "Contents-6th". You can easily change the look of your table of contents by changing the style definitions for these built-in "Contents" styles.

Creating an index

An **index** is a valuable reader aid in a longer document such as a report or manual. The Index Wizard helps you create an index with **main entries** and **subentries**, based on **index entry marks** you insert in frame, table, or artistic text.

To mark index entries:

1. Select a portion of text or click for an insertion point before the first word you want to mark.

2. Select **Edit Story** from the **Edit** menu. The WritePlus window opens.

3. Click the [⌂] **Mark Index** button on the Story toolbar.

4. Use the **Mark Index Entry** dialog to edit index entry marks in the Main entry or Subentry box.

If you selected a word or phrase in the story, it appears as the Main entry in the dialog. You can use the entry as it is, or type new text for the main entry and Sub-entry (if any). You must include a main entry for each sub-entry.

5. Click **Mark** to insert the new entry mark or update a selected mark.

> Index entry marks are invisible on the PagePlus screen and can only be added or edited in WritePlus.

To build an index:

1. First mark the entries as described above.

2. Choose **Index...** from the **Insert** menu.

3. Run through the Index Wizard, choosing where to place and how to format your index. Repeat at any time to update the information.

Producing a book with BookPlus

BookPlus is a management utility built into PagePlus that lets you produce a whole book from a set of separate PagePlus (*.ppp) publication files. Using BookPlus, you can arrange the chapter files in a specific order, systematically renumber pages, synchronize styles and other elements between all chapters, create a Table of Contents and/or Index for the whole book, and output the book via printing, PostScript®, or PDF. BookPlus can perform all these managerial tasks whether or not the original files are open! Your settings are saved as a compact BookPlus (*.ppb) book file, separate from the source publication files.

Working with books and chapters

A book consists of a set of PagePlus (*.ppp) publication files. Each publication file is considered a chapter in the book. To create a new book, you'll need at least one constituent chapter file.

To create a new book:

- In PagePlus, on the **File** menu, choose **New** and then click **New Book...**.

BookPlus opens with an empty dialog reserved for the **chapter list**.

To add a chapter to the chapter list:

1. In BookPlus, on the **Standard** toolbar, click 📷 **Add....**

2. In the dialog, select one or more PagePlus files to be added as chapters. (Use the **Ctrl** or **Shift** keys to select multiple files or a range of files.) Click **Open**.

The selected files appear in the chapter list, which can be reordered by dragging.

> 🖎 Once you've created a chapter list, you can add new chapters at any time, or replace/remove chapters in the current list from the **Standard** toolbar.

To save the current chapter list as a book file:

• Choose 💾 **Save** (or **Save As...**) from the BookPlus **Standard** toolbar.

> 🖎 You can open saved book files from PagePlus using **File>Open....** You can have more than one book file open at a time.

Numbering pages

BookPlus provides a variety of options for incrementing page numbers continuously from one chapter to another, through the whole book. Page numbers will only appear on pages or (more commonly) master pages where you've inserted page number fields. To "suppress" page numbers—for example, on a title page—simply don't include a page number field there.

BookPlus lets you change page number style choices you've made in the original file (using **Format/Page Number Format...** in PagePlus), and provides other options such as inserting a blank page when necessary to force new chapters to start on a right-hand page. You don't need to have the original files open to update page numbering.

To set page numbering options for the book:

1. Choose **Book Page Number Options...** from the BookPlus **File** menu.

2. In the dialog, select whether you want page numbers to **Continue from previous chapter**, **Continue on next odd page**, or **Continue on next even page**. Typically you'll want new chapters to start on odd (right-hand or "recto") pages.

3. Leave **Insert blank page when necessary** checked if you want to output an extra page at the end of a chapter where the next page number (if you've selected odd- or even-page continuation) would otherwise skip a page. Either way, BookPlus will number your pages correctly—but for correct imposition in professional printing it's usually best to insert the blank page. **Note:** You won't see the blank page inserted into your original file, only in the generated output.

4. Click **OK**. BookPlus immediately applies your settings to all chapters.

To set page numbering options for a chapter:

1. Select its name in the list and choose **Chapter Page Number Options...** from the Chapter menu.

The **Page Number Format** dialog displays current settings for numbering style and initial numbering for the chapter (or for any sections created within that chapter if you want to use mixed page number formats per section). (See Using page numbering on p. 59 for more details.)

If you've reordered chapters or changed the chapter list in any way, you can quickly reimpose correct numbering on the current list.

To update page numbering:

- Choose **Renumber Pages** from the BookPlus File menu.

Synchronizing chapters

Synchronizing means imposing consistent styles, palettes, and/or colour schemes throughout the book. This is accomplished by using one chapter (called the **style source**) as a model for the rest of the book. You define attributes in the style source chapter, and then select which attributes should be adjusted in other chapters to conform to the style source.

To set one chapter as the style source:

- Select its name in the chapter list and choose **Set Style Source** from the Chapter menu.

The current style source is identified in the Synchronized column of the chapter list.

To synchronize one or more chapters with the style source:

1. To update just certain chapters, make sure their names are selected in the chapter list.

2. Choose **Synchronize...** from the **File** menu.

3. In the dialog, select whether you want to update **All** or just **Selected** chapters. Check which attributes should be updated to conform to those defined in the style source file: **Text styles**, **Object styles**, **Colour scheme**, and/or **Colour palette**.

4. Click **OK**.

BookPlus imposes the specified changes and updates the Synchronized time in the chapter list for each selected file. If the file was altered in any way, the Modified time updates as well.

Building a Table of Contents or Index

From BookPlus, you can build a **Table of Contents** and/or **Index** that includes entries for the entire set of chapters.

To create a table of contents or index for the book:

1. In the chapter list, select the name of the chapter file where you want to add the table of contents or index.

2. Choose **Insert** from the Chapter menu and select **Table of Contents...** or **Index...** from the submenu.

BookPlus opens the chapter file if it's not already open, and the Wizard for the procedure you've selected appears.

3. Select **Yes** when the Wizard asks if you want to build a table of contents or index for the entire book. Continue clicking **Next>** and selecting choices in the Wizard.

Printing and PDF output

When you **print** or generate **PDF output** from BookPlus, you'll can print the entire book or selected chapters, including all, odd, or even pages.

To print or create a PDF from the book or selected chapters:

1. (Optional) To print just certain chapters, make sure their names are selected in the chapter list.

2. Choose   **Print Book** or   **Publish as PDF** from the BookPlus **Standard** toolbar.

For printing, set other options as detailed on p. 245, then click **Print**. For PDF output, set options as detailed on p. 255, then click **OK**.

Hyperlinking an object

Hyperlinking an object such as a box, Quick Button, a word, or a picture means that a reader of your PDF document (or visitor to your website) can trigger an event by clicking on the object. The event might be a jump to a different page, the appearance of an email composition window, the display of a graphic, text, or media file, or a jump to an anchor (p. 83) attached to a target object.

To hyperlink an object:

1. Use the **Pointer Tool** to highlight the region of text, or select an object.

2. Click   **Hyperlink** on the **Standard** toolbar.

3. In the **Hyperlinks** dialog, click to select the link destination type, and enter the specific hyperlink target—an Internet page, a page in your publication/website, an email address, local file, or an object's anchor on p. 83.

4. Click **OK**.

As a visual cue, hyperlinked words are underlined and appear in the colour you've specified in the Colour Scheme Designer.

To modify or remove a hyperlink:

- From the **Hyperlinks** dialog, which opens with the current link target shown, either:

    - To modify the hyperlink, select a new link destination type and/or target.

    - To remove the hyperlink, click the **Remove** button.

> For a "birds-eye" view of all the hyperlinks in your publication, use the **Hyperlink Manager** (**Tools** menu).

Viewing hyperlinks in your publication

The **Hyperlink Manager** gives you an overview of all the hyperlinks in your publication.

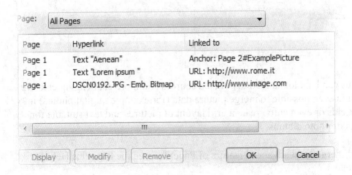

To display the Hyperlink Manager:

- Choose **Hyperlink Manager...** from the **Tools** menu.

The Hyperlink Manager dialog displays both object and text hyperlinks in your publication, listed by page number. The entries show each link's source object type (Text, Embedded bitmap, etc.) and its destination page, anchor name, or URL

To display a hyperlink for closer inspection:

- Click to select the link entry and click the **Display** button.

To remove or modify a hyperlink:

- Click to select the link entry and click the **Remove** or **Modify** button.
  To modify the hyperlink, select a new link destination type and/or
  target.

Using mail merge

Most commonly, **mail merge** means printing your publication a number of
times, inserting different information each time from a **data source** such as an
address list file—for example into a series of letters or mailing labels.

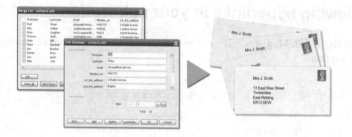

PagePlus can handle many kinds of data sources and more challenging creative
tasks. It is even possible to merge picture data (for example, digital photos) into
single fields or even auto-create a grid layout of pictures and text suitable for
catalogs or photo albums.

As mail merge is an advanced feature of PagePlus, see the PagePlus Help for
more details.

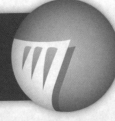

6 Pictures, Lines, and Shapes

Adding picture frames

Not to be confused with a decorative border, a **picture frame** is a shaped container similar to a text frame. You can select either:

- **Bordered** picture frames from the Gallery tab.

  - or -

- **Shaped** borderless frames from the **Tools** toolbar.

Either option lets you import a picture directly into the frame or drag a picture into it from the Media bar. Empty picture frames are shown as envelope-shaped placeholders. At any time you can replace the picture in the frame.

All selected picture frames that contain a picture will display a supporting **Picture frame** toolbar under the frame. This offers panning, rotation (90 degrees anti-clockwise), zoom in, zoom out, and replace picture controls).

To add a bordered picture frame:

1. From the Gallery tab, select **Picture Frames** in the drop-down list.

2. Scroll to a sub-category (e.g., Metallic, Natural, Masonry) of your choice.

3. Drag the frame design thumbnail to your page.

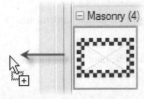

> Feel like a different picture frame? Simply drag another frame design from the tab at any time.

To add a borderless picture frame:

1. For an empty square frame, choose **Picture>Empty Frame...** from the **Insert** menu.
    - or -
    For a frame of a particular shape, e.g. Elliptical Picture Frame, choose a shape on the [icon] Picture Frames flyout on the **Tools** toolbar.

2. [icon] The mouse pointer changes to the **Picture Paste** cursor. What you do next determines the initial size and placement of the picture frame.

3. To insert the frame at a default size, simply click the mouse.
    - or -
    To set the size of the frame, drag out a region and release the mouse button. If needed, use the **Shift** key while dragging to maintain aspect ratio.

To add a picture to a frame:

*   From the Media bar's currently displayed album, drag and drop a photo directly onto the picture frame.
    - or -
    Click [icon] **Replace Picture** directly under the selected frame, locate and select an image. Click **Open**.

The picture is added to the frame using default Picture Frame properties, i.e. it is scaled to maximum fit; aspect ratio is always maintained. However, you can alter the picture's size, orientation and positioning relative to its frame.

To change picture size and positioning:

Select a populated picture frame, and from the toolbar underneath:

*   Click the [icon] button to position the photo in the picture frame by panning.

- Click the ⬚ button to rotate the photo in 90 degree anti-clockwise increments.

- Click the ⬚⬚ buttons to zoom in/out of the photo.

- or -

1. Right-click on a picture frame and choose **Properties>Frame Properties...**.
   - or -

   Select the picture frame and choose ⬚ **Frame Properties** on the Picture context toolbar.

2. In the dialog, you can scale to maximum/minimum, **Stretch to Fit**, or use the original image's size (**No Scale**).

3. To change vertical alignment of pictures within the frames, select **Top**, **Middle**, or **Bottom**.

4. For horizontal alignment, select **Left**, **Centre**, or **Right**.

While you can take advantage of PagePlus's preset frames you can create your own shape (e.g., a morphed QuickShape or closed curve) then convert it to a picture frame.

Creating custom picture frames

1. Create the shape as required.

2. Right-click the shape and select **Convert To>Picture Frame**.

You can then add a picture to the frame as described previously.

Importing pictures

PagePlus lets you insert pictures from a wide variety of file formats, including bitmaps, vector images, and metafiles, and in several different ways. Here's a quick overview:

- **Bitmapped pictures**, also known as **bitmaps** or **raster pictures**, are built from a matrix of dots ("pixels"), rather like the squares on a sheet of graph paper. They may originate as digital camera photos or scanned pictures, or be created (or enhanced) with a "paint" program or photo editor. Typical examples include gif, jpg, png, and .wdp.

- **Draw** graphics, also known as **vector images**, are resolution-independent and contain drawing commands such as "draw a line from A to B."

- **Metafiles** are the native graphics format for Windows and combine raster and vector information. Serif also has its own **Serif MetaFile Format (SMF)** which is optimized for image sharing between Serif applications.

You can also acquire pictures directly from PhotoCDs or via TWAIN devices (scanners or digital cameras)—see PagePlus Help.

Export objects to picture by using **File>Export As Picture...**.

Inserting pictures

To insert a picture into PagePlus you can copy and paste it, drag a file from an external Windows folder directly onto your page, drag a thumbnail from PagePlus's Media bar, or import a picture as an embedded or linked image via a dialog... even place it into a picture frame.

Bordered and unbordered shaped **picture frames** (p. 175) are a great way to present pictures that can be positioned and cropped within the frame. Drag the former from the Gallery tab; add the latter from the **Tools** toolbar. You can crop unframed pictures too (p. 79).

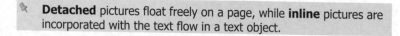

Detached pictures float freely on a page, while **inline** pictures are incorporated with the text flow in a text object.

To import a picture from a file:

1. To place the picture:

   - inline with the text - click for an insertion point in a text object.

   - detached from the text - make sure all text objects are deselected.

   - into a frame - create the frame (see above) and then select it.

2. *In the main window:*

   Click the ▦ **Import Picture...** button on the **Tools** toolbar's Picture flyout.

   In WritePlus:

   Choose **Picture File...** from the **Insert** menu.

   For frames:

   Click the ▦ **Replace Picture** button on the Picture Context toolbar.

3. Use the dialog to select the picture to open.

4. Select either **Embed Picture** or **Link Picture** to include or exclude the picture from the project, respectively. Use linked pictures to minimize project file size. (See Embedding vs. Linking on p. 180).

5. If you select the **Place at native dpi** option and the picture has a different internal setting, PagePlus will scale it accordingly; otherwise it applies a screen resolution setting of **96 dpi**. Either way—or if you resize it downwards later on—the picture retains all its original picture data until it's published. Check **Place as raster** if you want to permanently convert an imported eps, Windows Metafile or Serif Metafile to a bitmap.

6. Click **Open**.

7. If there's a text insertion point in the current text frame story and the picture is too large for the frame, you'll be prompted whether to shrink it down. Click **Yes** if you want to do this or click **No** to insert it at a default size.

If there was no text insertion point, ⬚ the mouse pointer changes to the **Picture Paste**. What you do next determines the initial size and placement of the detached picture.

- To insert the picture at a default size, simply click the mouse.
  - or -

- To set the size of the inserted picture, drag out a region and release the mouse button.

To populate a template picture placeholder or replace a picture:

- Click the 🖉 button shown under the selected frame.
  - or -

- Double-click the placeholder/picture.

Embedding vs. linking

Embedding means the picture in PagePlus is now distinct from the original file. Embedding results in a larger PagePlus file, and if you need to alter an embedded picture you'll need to re-import it after editing. Still, it's the best choice if file size isn't an issue and graphics are final.

Linking inserts a copy of the picture file into the PagePlus publication, linked to the actual file so that any changes you later make to it in the native application will be automatically reflected in PagePlus.

Using the Media Bar

The Media Bar acts as a "basket" containing photos for inclusion in your publication. Its chief use is to aid the design process by improving efficiency (avoiding having to import photos one by one) and convenience (making photos always-at-hand). For photo-rich documents in particular, the Media Bar is a valuable tool for dragging photos directly into picture frames or for simply replacing existing pictures on the page.

You can even use the **AutoFlow** feature to add all photos sequentially into available empty picture frames with one click.

The bar can be used as a temporary storage area before placing photos in your document, or it can be used to create more permanent photo albums from which you can retrieve stored photos at any time. By default, photos are added to a **temporary album** but remember to click the New Album button if you want to save your album for later use. Each time you start PagePlus you simply load that saved album (or any other saved album) or just work with a temporary album—the choice is yours!

Photo albums can be subsequently modified, renamed and deleted—viewing the contents of an individual album or all albums at the same time is possible.

You can import an unlimited number of photos by file or by whole folders, and set photo resolution (native or 96dpi) and whether photos are embedded or linked to your project in advance of photo placement on the page.

For large photo collections, searching throughout albums for photos by file name and EXIF, IPTC or XMP metadata is possible in the search box at the top of the Media Bar; even edit XMP metadata from within PagePlus.

> ✎ The currently loaded album shown on your Media Bar will remain visible irrespective of which document you have open.

Photo thumbnails can be dragged from the Media Bar directly onto your page, as an existing standalone photo, or into an empty or populated picture frame.

To view the Media Bar:

- Unless already displayed, click the ▬▬▲▬▬ handle at the bottom of your workspace.

To add photos to a temporary album:

1. With the Media Bar visible and a temporary album loaded, click on the Media Bar's workspace to reveal an **Import Picture** dialog.

2. From the dialog, navigate to a photo or folder, and select your photo(s).

3. Click **Open**. Your photos appear as thumbnails in the Menu Bar workspace.

> ✎ Unless you save it, the temporary album and its photo contents will not be saved when you close PagePlus.
>
> ♡ You can drag one or more files from any Windows folder directly into the Media Bar window. To save a temporary album to a named album:

1. Click the down arrow on the 🖳 **Add To** button. From the menu, select **New Album**.

2. In the **New Album** dialog, in the **Album Name** box, type a name to identify your album in the future.

3. (Optional) For any photo you can alter the resolution (native or 96 dpi), or embed/link status in advance of placement on your page—click a photo's setting and use the setting's drop-down menu to change. You can also change these settings during drag/drop onto the page.

4. Click **OK**.

To include a temporary album's photos in an existing saved album, click the **Add To** button and choose a named album from the menu.

To load a saved album:

- Select a saved album name from the bar's top-right drop-down menu. The album's photos will display in the workspace.

To rename or delete an album:

- Right-click an existing album name in the top-right drop-down menu and choose **Rename Album...** or **Delete Album...**.

To sort photos in your album:

- In the **Sort By** search box, select a sorting criteria. Files will be rearranged according to the chosen criteria (by Filename, Rating, or Date Taken).

Adding photos to the page

To add a photo to your page:

1. Display the Media Bar's temporary album or load a saved album from the top-right drop-down menu.

2. Drag an album's photo thumbnail onto the page—either as a detached photo, or directly into a picture frame.
   - or -
   Use the **AutoFlow** feature.

AutoFlow—adding content automatically

AutoFlow lets you flow the photos currently displayed in the Media Bar throughout empty picture **frames** spread throughout your publication (you can't reflow photos once frames are populated with content). This is especially useful when using Photo Album design templates or other photo-rich documents.

To use this feature, you must have multiple picture frames present in your current document, as well as a range of photos present in your Media Bar. The autoflow process involves a simple click of the mouse button.

To automatically flow your photos:

- Click the **AutoFlow** button to the right of the bar's workspace. The photos are placed sequentially in your document's available picture frames in the order they appear in the Media Bar.

Using Image Cutout Studio

Image Cutout Studio offers a powerful integrated solution for cutting objects out from their backgrounds. Depending on the make up of your images you can separate subject of interests from their backgrounds, either by retaining the subject of interest (usually people, objects, etc.) or removing a simple uniform background (e.g., sky, studio backdrop). In both instances, the resulting "cutout" image creates an eye-catching look for your publication.

The latter background removal method is illustrated in the following multi-image example.

The white initial background is discarded, leaving interim checkerboard transparency, from which another image can be used as a more attractive background. A red tint on the second image's background is used to indicate areas to be discarded.

To launch Image Cutout Studio:

1. Select an image to be cut out.

2. Select ![icon] **Image Cutout Studio** from the displayed Picture context toolbar. Image Cutout Studio is launched.

Choose an output

It's essential that you choose an output type prior to selecting areas for keeping/discarding. Either an alpha-edged or vector-cropped bitmap can be chosen as your output type prior to selection. The choice you make really depends on the image, in particular how well defined image edges are.

Zoom into your image to examine its edges; this may influence the output type chosen.

Let's look at the output types and explain the difference between each.

Output Type	Description and use
Alpha-edged Bitmap	Use when cutting out objects with poorly defined edges. Transparency and pixel blending are used at the outline edge to produce professional results with negligible interference from background colours. The term "alpha" refers to a 32-bit image's alpha transparency channel.
Vector-cropped Bitmap	Use on more well-defined edges. A cropped image with crop outline is created which can be later manipulated with the crop tools. You can optionally apply feathering to the image edge but will not remove background colour.

You can also set the level of transparency and pixel blending at the cutout edge by adjusting the output settings, Width and Blur. Control of the cutout edge lets you blend your cutout into new backgrounds more realistically.

To create an alpha-edged bitmap:

1. Select **Alpha-edged Bitmap** from the **Output Type** drop-down menu.

2. (Optional) Drag the **Width** slider to set the extent to which the "alpha" blending is applied inside the cutout edge. This creates an offset region within which blending occurs.

3. (Optional) Adjust the **Blur** slider to apply a level of smoothing to the region created by the above Width setting.

To create a vector-cropped bitmap:

1. Select **Vector-cropped Bitmap** from the **Output Type** drop-down menu.

2. (Optional) Drag the **Feather** slider to apply a soft or blurry edge inside the cutout edge.

3. (Optional) Drag the **Smoothness** slider to smooth out the cutout edge.

4. (Optional) The **Inflate** slider acts as an positive or negative offset from the cutout edge.

> You'll need to click **Preview** in order to check output setting adjustments each time.

Selecting areas to keep or discard

A pair of brushes for keeping and discarding is used to "paint" areas of the image. The tools are called **Keep Brush** and **Discard Brush**, and are either used independently or, more typically, in combination with each other. When using either tool, the brush paints an area contained by an outline which is considered to be retained or discarded (depending on brush type). A configurable number of pixels adjacent to the outline area are blended.

To aid the selection operation, several display modes are available to show selection.

Show Original, **Show Tinted**, and **Show Transparent** buttons respectively display the image with:

- selection areas only.

- various coloured tints aiding complex selection operations.

- checkerboard transparency areas marked for discarding.

For Show tinted, a red tint indicates areas to be discarded; a green tint shows areas to be kept.

Background colour

For Show transparent mode, a different **Background colour** can be set (at bottom of the Studio) which might help differentiate areas to keep or discard.

To select image areas for keeping/discarding:

1. In Image Cutout Studio, click either **Keep Brush Tool** or **Discard Brush Tool** from the left of the Studio workspace.

2. (Optional) Pick a **Brush size** suitable for the area to be worked on.

3. (Optional) Set a **Grow Tolerance** value to automatically expand the selected area under the cursor (by detecting colours similar to those within the current selection). The greater the value the more the selected area will grow. Uncheck the option to switch the feature off.

4. Using the circular cursor, click and drag across the area to be retained or discarded (depending on Keep or Discard Brush Tool selection). It's OK to repeatedly click and drag until your selection area is made.

   The **Undo** button reverts to the last made selection.

> To fine-tune your selection, you can switch between Keep and Discard brushes by temporarily holding down the **Alt** key.

5. If you're outputting an alpha-edged bitmap, you can refine the area to be kept/discarded within Image Cutout Studio (only after previewing) with Erase and Restore touch-up tools. Vector-cropped images can be cropped using standard PagePlus crop tools outside of the Studio.

> Make your outline edge as exact as possible by using brush and touch-up tools before committing your work.

6. Click **OK** to create your cutout.

You'll see your image in your publication in its original location, but with the selected areas cut away (made transparent).

> Click **Reset** if you want to revert your selected areas and start your cutout again.

Refining your cutout area (alpha-edged bitmaps only)

If a vector-cropped image is created via Image Cutout Studio it's possible to subsequently manipulate the crop outline using crop tools. However, for alpha-edged bitmaps, Erase and Restore touch-up tools can be used to refine the cutout area within the Studio before completing your cutout. The latter can't be edited with crop tools.

> The touch-up tools are brush based and are only to be used to fine-tune your almost complete cutout—use your Keep and Discard brush tools for the bulk of your work!

To restore or remove portions of your cutout:

1. With your cutout areas already defined, click **Preview** (Output settings tab). You can use the button to check your cutout as you progress.

2. Click the ✐ **Restore Touch-up Tool** or ✐ **Erase Touch-up Tool** button from the left of the Studio workspace.

3. Paint the areas for restoring or erasing as you would with the brush tools.

4. Click ✅.

> If you've touched up part of your image between each preview, you'll be asked if you want to save or discard changes.

Applying PhotoLab filters

Filters can be applied and managed in **PhotoLab**, a powerful studio for applying adjustment and effect filters to pictures individually or in combination—all instantly applied and previewed! PhotoLab offers the following key features:

- **Adjustment filters**
  Apply tonal, colour, lens, and sharpening filters.

- **Effect filters**
  Apply distortion, blur, stylistic, noise, render, artistic and various other effects.

- **Retouching filters**
  Apply red eye correction, spot repair, straightening, and cropping.

- **Non-destructive operation**
  All filters are applied without affecting the original picture, and can be edited at any point in the future.

- **Powerful filter combinations**
  Create combinations of mixed adjustment, retouching, and effect filters for savable workflows.

- **Selective masking**
  Apply filters to selected regions using masks.

- **Save and manage favourites**
  Save filter combinations to a handy **Favourites** tab.

- **Viewing controls**
  Compare before-and-after previews, with dual- and split-screen controls. Use pan and zoom control for moving around your picture.

- **Locking controls**
  Protect your applied filters from accidental change, then optionally apply them to other images on selection.

PhotoLab hosts filter tabs, a main toolbar, and applied filter stack around a central workspace.

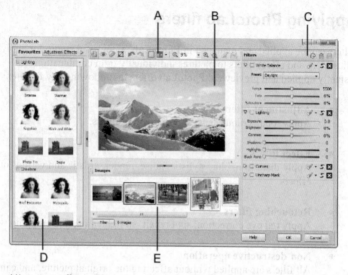

(A) main toolbar, (B) main workspace, (C) filter stack,
(D) filter tabs, (E) Images tab

To launch PhotoLab:

1. Select the picture that you want to apply a filter to.

2. Click ⬤ **PhotoLab** on the Picture context toolbar.

Using the Images tab

Pictures present in your publication will show in your **Images** tab (above) if the tab is expanded. This tab is shown by default in PhotoLab and can be hidden by clicking the ▬▬▼▬▬ button at the bottom of your workspace.

To search publication images:

1. Click the **Filter** button on the **Images** tab.

2. Select and define a minimum and maximum size, if required.

3. Select/deselect RGB, CMYK and Greyscale to filter by colour mode.

4. Click **OK**.

Applying a filter

Filters are stored in PhotoLab's Favourites, Adjustments, and Effects tabs which group filters logically into categories (e.g., Quick Fix for fast and commonly used correction filters).

The Favourites tab offers some commonly used filters (individual and in combination). You can complement these with your own user-defined filters.

To apply a filter with trialling:

1. Click a filter thumbnail.

2. As soon as a filter is selected it is temporarily added to **Trial Zone** which lets you experiment freely with your own settings for that filter; the picture automatically refreshes to preview your new settings.

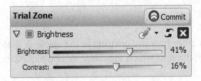

3. Adjust sliders (or enter input values) until your filter suits your requirements. Some filters offer check boxes, drop-down menus, and additional controls (e.g., Advanced settings).

> Selecting a new filter always replaces the current filter.

Any filter can be temporarily disabled, reset, or deleted from the trial zone.

To disable: Click ■, then click ☐ to enable again.

To reset: Click ↻ . Any changes to settings are reverted back to
the filter's defaults.

To delete: Click ❌.

Once you're sure that you want to keep your filter, you'll need to commit the
filter to your filters stack.

To commit your filter:

- Click ⊙ **Commit** to accept your changes. This adds the filter to the
  right-most **Filters** stack where additional filters can be added and built
  up by using the same method.

> ✎ Adjustments are applied such that the most recently added filter
> always appears at the bottom of the list and is applied to the picture
> last (after the other filters above it).

To reorder filters:

- Drag and drop your filter into any position in the stack. A dotted line
  indicates the new position in which the entry will be placed on mouse
  release.

To add a filter directly (without trialling):

- Click ⊞ **Add Quick Filter** at the top of the Filters stack and choose
  a filter from the flyout categories. The filter is applied directly to the
  stack without trialling.

Retouching

PhotoLab offers some useful retouching tools on the main toolbar, each
commonly used to correct photos before applying colour correction and effects.

Selective masking

Rather than apply a filter to uniformly change the appearance of your picture, you can change only selected regions instead. PhotoLab lets you mask picture areas by painting areas to be either affected by filters or simply left alone.

To apply a mask:

1. From the 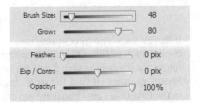 **Mask** drop-down menu, select **New Mask**.

2. In the Tool Settings pane, select the **Add Region** tool to allow you to mask regions by painting.

3. Adjust the settings to suit requirements, especially adjusting Brush Size to paint larger or more intricate regions.

Brush Size:		48
Grow:		80
Feather:		0 pix
Exp / Contr:		0 pix
Opacity:		100%

⭐ Change the **Mode** drop-down menu from Select to Protect to protect painted regions from masking (i.e., the inverse of the Add Region option).

4. Using the on-screen cursor, paint regions (in green for adding; red for protecting).

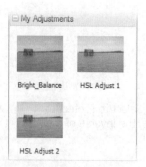
    If you've not been as accurate as you'd like while painting, you can click **Remove Regions** then paint over the unwanted painted regions.

5. Click ![icon] to save your masking changes.

It's also possible to create additional masks for the same filter as above, and then choose between masks accordingly. You can only have one mask applied at any one time. By using the menu's **New From>** option you can also base the new mask on another mask applied to the current or any other filter in the filter stack. This is useful when using favourites containing multiple adjustments.

To edit a mask:

*   Click the down arrow on the ![icon] button, choose the mask name and select **Edit Mask**.

Saving favourites

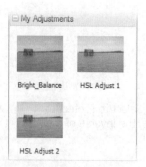

If there's a specific filter setting (or combination of filters) you want to keep for future use it's easy to save it as a **favourite**. PhotoLab stores all your favourites together in the Favourites tab. You can even create your own categories (e.g. My Adjustments) within the tab.

To save filter(s) as a new favourite:

- Click **Save Filter**.

- From the dialog, enter a favourite name and pick a category to save the filter to. (Click ☐ to create new category)

If you want to further manage your favourites into user-defined categories, click the option on the ▷ **Tab Menu**.

Importing TWAIN images

If your scanner or digital camera provides **TWAIN** support, you can import pictures directly into PagePlus using the TWAIN standard. Or, save the scanned image separately and then import into PagePlus.

To set up your TWAIN device for importing:

- See the documentation supplied with your scanner for operating instructions.

To import a scanned image:

- Choose **Picture...** from the **Insert** menu, then select **TWAIN** and **Acquire...** from the submenu to open a file selection dialog.

If you have more than one TWAIN-compatible device installed, you may need to select which source you wish to scan with.

To select a different TWAIN source for scanning:

1. Choose **Picture...** from the **Insert** menu, then select **TWAIN** and **Select Source** from the submenu.

2. Identify the device you want to use as your TWAIN source.

Drawing and editing lines

PagePlus provides **Pencil**, **Straight Line**, and **Pen** tools for drawing freehand, straight, and curved/straight lines, respectively.

The ✎ **Pencil Tool** lets you sketch curved lines and shapes in a freeform way.

The ＼ **Straight Line Tool** is for drawing straight lines (for example, drawn in the column gutter to separate columns); rules at the top and/or bottom of the page; or horizontal lines to separate sections or highlight headlines.

The ✒ **Pen Tool** lets you join a series of line segments (which may be curved or straight) using "connect the dots" mouse clicks.

Drawing lines

To draw a freeform line (with the Pencil Tool):

1. Choose the ✎ **Pencil Tool** from the **Tools** toolbar's Line flyout.

2. Click where you want the line to start, and hold the mouse button down as you draw. The line appears immediately and follows your mouse movements.

3. To end the line, release the mouse button. The line will automatically smooth out.

4. To extend the line, position the cursor over one of its square end nodes. The cursor changes to include a plus symbol. Click on the node and drag to add a new line segment.

To draw a straight line (with the Straight Line Tool):

1. Choose the **Straight Line Tool** from the **Tools** toolbar's Line flyout.

2. Click where you want the line to start, and drag to the end point. The line appears immediately.

> To constrain the angle of the straight line to 15° increments, hold down the **Shift** key as you drag. (This is an easy way to make exactly vertical or horizontal lines.)

3. To extend the line, position the cursor over one of its end nodes. The cursor changes to include a plus symbol. Click on the node and drag to add a new line segment.

To draw one or more line segments (with the Pen Tool):

1. Choose the **Pen Tool** from the **Tools** toolbar's Line flyout. On the Curve context toolbar, three buttons let you select which kind of segment to draw:

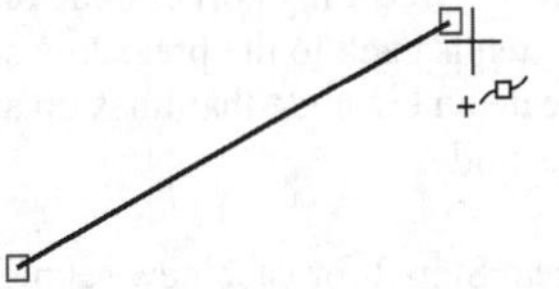

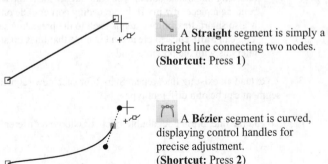

A **Straight** segment is simply a straight line connecting two nodes. (**Shortcut:** Press **1**)

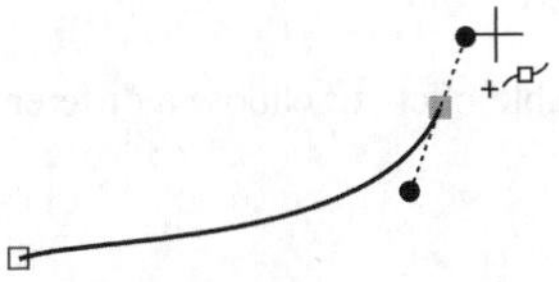

A **Bézier** segment is curved, displaying control handles for precise adjustment. (**Shortcut:** Press **2**)

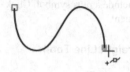

Smart segments appear without visible control handles, using automatic curve-fitting to connect each node. They are especially useful when tracing around curved objects and pictures. (**Shortcut:** Press **3**)

2. Select a segment type, then click where you want the line to start:

    - For a **Straight** segment, click again (or drag) for a new node where you want the segment to end. **Shift**-click to align the segment at 15° intervals (useful for quick right-angle junctions).

    - For a **Bézier** segment, click again for a new node and drag out a **control handle** from it. Control handles act like "magnets," pulling the curve into shape. The distance between handles determines the depth of the resulting new curved line segment.

      Click again where you want the segment to end, and a curved segment appears. The finished segment becomes selectable.

    - For a **Smart** segment, click again for a new node. The segment appears as a smooth, best-fitting curve (without visible control handles) between the new node and the preceding node. Before releasing the mouse button, you can drag to "flex" the line as if bending a piece of wire. If the preceding corner node on the line is also smart, flexibility extends back to the preceding segment. You can **Shift**-click to create a new node that lines up at 15° intervals with the previous node.

3. To extend an existing line, repeat Step 2 for each new segment. Each segment can be of a different type.

4. To end the line, press **Esc**, double-click, or choose a different tool.

Editing lines

Use the Pointer Tool in conjunction with the Curve context toolbar to adjust lines once you've drawn them. The techniques are the same whether you're editing a separate line object or the outline of a closed shape.

When selected, each line type shows square nodes which can be used for reshaping lines.

See PagePlus Help for information on editing lines.

Setting line properties

All lines, including those that enclose shapes, have numerous properties, including colour, weight (width or thickness), scaling, cap (end), join (corner), and stroke alignment. You can vary these properties for any freehand, straight, or curved line, as well as for the outline of a shape. Note that text frames, pictures, tables, and artistic text objects have line properties, too.

In PagePlus, you can control the position of the stroke (i.e., line width) in relation to the object's path, i.e. the line that defines the boundary of the object.

To change line properties of a selected object:

- Use the ▬ **Line** swatch on the **Swatches tab** to change the line's colour and/or shade. Alternatively, use the equivalent swatch on the Colour tab to apply a line colour from a colour mixer.

- Use the **Line** tab, context toolbar (shown when a line is selected), or Line and Border dialog to change the line's weight (thickness), type, or other properties. Select a line width, and use the drop-down boxes to pick the type of line. The context toolbar can also adjust line-end scaling as a percentage.

On the Line tab, context toolbar, or Line and Border dialog, the styles drop-down menu provides the following styles: **None**, **Single**, **Calligraphic**, and several **Dashed** and **Double** line styles as illustrated below.

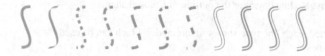

Several techniques offer additional ways to customize lines:

For dotted/dashed lines, select from one of five dashed line styles (see above).
- or -
(tab and dialog only) Drag the **Dash Pattern** slider to set the overall pattern length (the number of boxes to the left of the slider) and the dash length (the number of those boxes that are black).

The illustrations below show lines with pattern and dash lengths of (1) 4 and 2, and (2) 5 and 4:

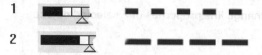

For double lines, select from one of four **Double** line styles (see above).

(Tab only) For calligraphic lines of variable width (drawn as if with a square-tipped pen held at a certain angle), select the calligraphic line style (opposite) from the drop-down menu, then use the **Calligraphic Angle** box to set the angle of the pen tip.

Choose a **Stroke Alignment** setting to fit the line's stroke to the middle, inside, or outside of the object's path (using Align Centre, Align Inner, or Align Outer buttons, respectively).

You can also vary a line's **Cap** (end) and the **Join** (corner) where two lines intersect.

Drawing and editing shapes

QuickShapes are pre-designed objects of widely varying shapes that you can instantly add to your page.

Once you've drawn a QuickShape, you can morph its original shape using control handles, and adjust its properties—for example, by applying gradient or bitmap fills (including your own bitmap pictures!) or transparency effects.

Another way to create a shape is to draw a line (or series of line segments) and then connect its start and end nodes, creating a closed shape.

QuickShapes

The QuickShape flyout contains a wide variety of commonly used shapes, including boxes, ovals, arrows, polygons, stars, cubes, and cylinders.

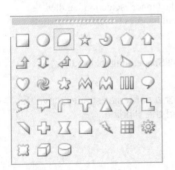

You can easily turn shapes into web **buttons** by adding hyperlinks or overlaying hotspots. The "Quick Button" (indicated) is especially intended for creating stylish button outlines!

It's also possible to use the always-at-hand QuickShape context toolbar situated above the workspace to swap QuickShapes, and adjust a QuickShape's line weight, colour, style, and more. New shapes always take the default line and fill (initially a black line with no fill).

To create a QuickShape:

1. Click the ▢ ▾ **QuickShape** flyout on the **Tools** toolbar and select a shape from the flyout. The button takes on the icon of the shape selected.

2. Click on the page to create a new shape at a default size.
   - or -

   Drag across the page to size your shape. When the shape is the right size, release the mouse button.

To draw a constrained shape (such as a circle):

- Hold down the **Shift** key as you drag.

All QuickShapes can be positioned, resized, rotated, and filled. What's more, you can morph them using adjustable sliding handles around the QuickShape. Each shape changes in a logical way to allow its exact appearance to be altered.

To adjust the appearance of a QuickShape:

1. Click on the QuickShape to reveal one or more sliding handles around the shape. These are distinct from the "inner" selection handles. Different QuickShapes have different handles which have separate functions.

2. To change the appearance of a QuickShape, drag its handles.

💡 To find out what each handle does for a particular shape, move the Pointer Tool over the handle and read the Hintline.

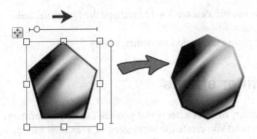

Closed shapes

As soon as you draw or select a line, you'll see the line's nodes appear. Nodes show the end points of each segment in the line. Freehand curves typically have many nodes; straight or curved line segments have only two. You can make a shape by extending a line back to its starting point.

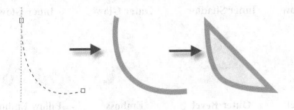

To turn a selected line into a shape:

- Select the line with the **Pointer Tool** and then click the **Close Curve** button on the Curve context toolbar.

You can go the other way, too—break open a shape in order to add one or more line segments.

To break open a line or shape:

1. With the **Pointer Tool**, select the node where you want to break the shape.

2. Click the **Break Curve** button on the Curve context toolbar. A line will separate into two lines. A shape will become a line, with the selected node split into two nodes, one at each end of the new line.

3. You can now use the **Pointer Tool** to reshape the line as needed.

See PagePlus Help for more information on editing shapes.

Applying 2D filter effects

PagePlus provides a variety of **filter effects** that you can use to transform any object. "3D" filter effects let you create the impression of a textured surface and are covered elsewhere (see p. 208). Here we'll look at 2D filter effects exclusively. The following examples show each 2D filter effect when applied to the letter "A."

Drop Shadow	Inner Shadow	Outer Glow	Inner Glow
Inner Bevel	Outer Bevel	Emboss	Pillow Emboss
Gaussian Blur	Zoom Blur	Radial Blur	Motion Blur
Colour Fill	Feather	Outline	Reflection

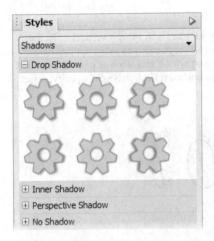

The Studio's Styles tab offers a range of 2D filter effects that are ready to use. Its multiple categories each offer a gallery full of predefined effects, such as Shadows, Bevels, Reflections, Blurs, and more. Each category offers subtle variations of the category effect. Click any thumbnail to apply the effect to the selected object.

PagePlus additionally provides the Shadow Tool for applying a shadow to an object directly in your publication (or website). Control handles let you adjust shadow blur, opacity and colour.

To apply 2D filter effects:

1. Select an object and click the *fx* **Filter Effects** button on the **Attributes** toolbar.

    - or -

    Choose **Filter Effects...** from the **Format** menu (or via the right-click menu). The Filter Effects dialog appears.

2. To apply a particular effect, check its box in the list at left.

3. To adjust the properties of a specific effect, select its name and vary the dialog controls. Adjust the sliders or enter specific values to vary the combined effect. (You can also select a slider and use the keyboard arrows.) Options differ from one effect to another.

4. Click **OK** to apply the effect or **Cancel** to abandon changes.

Creating reflections

A simple way to add creative flair to your page is to apply a vertical reflection on a selected object. The effect is especially eye-catching when applied to pictures, but can be equally impressive on artistic text, such as page titles or text banners. A combination of settings can control reflection height, opacity, offset and blurring.

Creating outlines

PagePlus lets you create a coloured outline around objects, especially text and shapes (as a **filter effect**). For any outline, you can set the outline width, colour fill, transparency, and blend mode. The outline can also take a gradient fill, a unique **contour** fill (fill runs from the inner to outer edge of the outline width), or pattern fill and can also sit inside, outside, or be centred on the object edge.

As with all effects you can switch the outline effect on and off. You'll be able to apply a combination of 2D or 3D filter effects along with your outline, by checking other options in the Filter Effects dialog.

Using the Shadow Tool

Shadows are great for adding flair and dimension to your work, particularly to pictures and text objects, but also to shapes, text frames and tables. To help you create them quickly and easily, PagePlus provides the **Shadow Tool** on the **Attributes** toolbar. The tool affords freeform control of the shadow effect allowing creation of adjustable **basic** or **skewed edge-based shadows** for any PagePlus object.

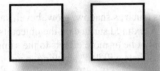

Basic (left) and skewed shadows (right) applied to a basic square QuickShape

Adjustment of shadow colour, opacity, blur, and scaling/distance is possible using controllable nodes directly on the page (or via a supporting Shadow context toolbar). Nodes can be dragged inwards or outwards from the shadow origin to modify the shadow's blur and opacity. For a different colour, pick a new colour from the Colour or Swatches tab while the tool is selected. Depending on if a basic or skewed shadow is required, the origin can exist in the centre (shown) or at the edge of an object, respectively.

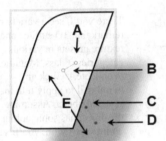

(A) Blur, (B) Shadow origin, (C) Opacity, (D) Colour, (E) Scaling

Once you've created a shadow, you can also fine-tune it as needed using the Filter Effects dialog.

Using 3D filter effects

3D filter effects go beyond 2D filter effects (such as shadow, glow, bevel, and emboss effects) to create the impression of a textured surface on the object itself. You can use the **Filter Effects** dialog to apply one or more effects to the same object. Keep in mind that none of these 3D effects will "do" anything to an unfilled object—you'll need to have a fill there to see the difference they make!

The Studio's Styles tab is a good place to begin experimenting with 3D filter effects. Its multiple categories each offers a gallery full of pre-defined mixed 2D and 3D effects, using various settings.

There you'll see a variety of remarkable 3D surface and texture presets in various categories (Glass, Metallic, Wood, etc.). Click any thumbnail to apply it to the selected object. Assuming the object has some colour on it to start with, you'll see an instant result!

fx   Alternatively, you can customize a Styles tab preset, or apply one or more specific effects from scratch, by using **Filter Effects** on the **Attributes** toolbar.

Overview

3D Bump Map
    Function
       Advanced
2D Bump Map
3D Pattern Map
    Function
       Advanced
2D Pattern Map
Reflection Map
Transparency
✔ 3D Lighting

- **3D Effects** is a master switch, and its settings of **Blur** and **Depth** make a great difference; you can click the "+" button to unlink them for independent adjustment.

- **3D Lighting** provides a "light source" without which any depth information in the effect wouldn't be visible. The lighting settings let you illuminate your 3D landscape and vary its reflective properties.

To apply 3D filter effects:

1. Click *fx* **Filter Effects** on the **Attributes** toolbar.

2. Check the **3D Effects** box at the left. The **3D Lighting** box is checked by default.

3. Adjust the "master control" sliders here to vary the overall properties of any individual 3D effects you select.

   - **Blur** specifies the amount of smoothing applied. Larger blur sizes give the impression of broader, more gradual changes in height.

   - **Depth** specifies how steep the changes in depth appear.

   - The ⊞ button is normally down, which links the two sliders so that sharp changes in Depth are smoothed out by the Blur parameter. To adjust the sliders independently, click the button so it's up.

4. Check a 3D effect in the 3D Effects list which reflects the 3D effect you can achieve.

3D Bump Map

The **3D Bump Map** effect creates the impression of a textured surface by applying a mathematical function you select to add depth information, for a peak-and-valley effect. You can use 3D Bump Map in conjunction with one or more additional 3D filter effects—but not with a 2D Bump Map.

2D Bump Map

The **2D Bump Map** effect creates the impression of a textured surface by applying a greyscale bitmap you select to add depth information, for a peak-and-valley effect. You can use 2D Bump Map in conjunction with one or more additional 3D filter effects—but not with a 3D Bump Map.

3D Pattern Map

The **3D Pattern Map** effect creates the impression of a textured surface by applying a mathematical function you select to introduce colour variations. You can use 3D Pattern Map in conjunction with one or more other 3D filter effects.

2D Pattern Map

The **2D Pattern Map** effect creates the impression of a textured surface by applying a greyscale bitmap you select to introduce colour variations. You can use 2D Pattern Map in conjunction with one or more other 3D filter effects.

Transparency

The uniform transparency of an object (with 3D filter effects applied) can be controlled via the Transparency tab (see first example below). However, for more sophisticated transparency control, especially for simulating reflective lighting effects on glass objects, transparency settings can instead be set within the 3D filter effects dialog (check the **Transparency** option). The effect can be used to create more realistic transparency by independently controlling transparency on reflective (edges) and non-reflective (flat) areas of the object (see front heart shape below).

3D Reflection Map

The **3D Reflection Map** effect is used to simulate mirrored surfaces by selection of a pattern (i.e., a bitmap which possesses a shiny surface) which "wraps around" a selected object. Patterns which simulate various realistic indoor and outdoor environments can be adopted, with optional use of 3D lighting to further reflect off object edges.

3D Lighting

The **3D Lighting** effect works in conjunction with other 3D effects to let you vary the surface illumination and reflective properties.

Adding dimensionality (Instant 3D)

Using the **Instant 3D** feature, you can easily transform flat shapes (shown) and text into three-dimensional objects.

PagePlus provides control over 3D effect settings such as:

- **bevelling**: use several rounded and chiseled presets or create your own with a custom bevel profile editor.

- **lighting**: up to eight editable and separately coloured lights can be positioned to produce dramatic lighting effects.

- **lathe effects**: create contoured objects (e.g., a bottle cork) with the custom lathe profile editor and extrusion control.

- **texture**: control how texture is extruded on objects with non-solid fills.

- **viewing**: rotate your object in three dimensions.

- **material**: controls the extent to which lighting has an effect on the object's surfaces (great for 3D artistic text!).

An always-at-hand 3D context toolbar hosted above your workspace lets you configure the above settings—each setting contributes to the 3D effect applied to the selected object. For on-the-page object control you can transform in 3D with use of a red orbit circle, which acts as an axis from which you can rotate around the X-, Y-, and Z-axes in relation to your page. Look for the cursor changing as you hover over the red circles' nodes or wire frame.

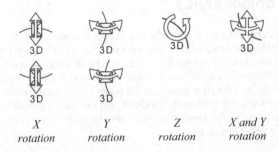

| *X* | *Y* | *Z* | *X and Y* |
| rotation | rotation | rotation | rotation |

Transform about your 3D objects' axes instead of your pages' axes by holding the **Ctrl** key down as you transform using the nodes.

You can also adjust the angle and elevation of each "active" light on the page by dragging the light pointer to a position which simulates a light source.

After any transformation, the underlying base object remains editable.

To add dimensionality:

1. Select an object and click the **Instant 3D** button on the **Attributes** toolbar. The object immediately adopts 3D characteristics with a red orbit circle displayed in the object's foreground.

2. Click a 3D effect category from the first drop-down menu on the 3D context toolbar; the bar's options change dynamically according to the category currently selected. See the PagePlus Help for more details.

Click **Reset Defaults** on the context toolbar to revert to the object back to its initial transformation.

To switch off 3D effects:

- Click **Remove 3D** on the context toolbar. You can always click the Attribute toolbar's **Instant 3D** button at any time later to reinstate the effect.

Using object styles

Object styles benefit your design efforts in much the same way as text styles and colour schemes. Once you've come up with a set of attributes that you like—properties like line colour, fill, border, and so on—you can save this cluster of attributes as a named style. PagePlus remembers which objects are using that style, and the style appears in the Styles tab, and can subsequently be applied to new objects. For example a Quick Star can have a stone effect applied via an object style you've saved previously (all object styles use a cog shape as the default object preview type).

Here's how object styles work to your advantage:

- Each object style can include settings for a host of object attributes, such as line colour, line style, fill, transparency, filter effects, font, and border. The freedom to include or exclude certain attributes, and the nearly unlimited range of choices for each attribute, makes this a powerful tool in the designer's arsenal.

- Any time you want to alter some aspect of a style (for example, change the line colour), you simply change the style definition. Instantly, all objects in your publication sharing that style update accordingly.

- Object styles you've saved globally appear not only in the original publication but in any new publication, so you can reuse exactly the same attractive combination of attributes for any subsequent design effort.

The **Styles tab** contains multiple galleries of pre-designed styles that you can apply to any object, or customize to suit your own taste! Galleries exist in effect categories such as Blurs, 3D, Edge, Warps, Shadows, Materials (e.g., metals) and more, with each category having further subcategories.

To apply an object style to one or more objects:

1. Display the **Styles** tab.

2. Expand the drop-down menu to select a named style category (e.g., Blurs), then pick a subcategory by scrolling the lower window.

3. Preview available styles as thumbnails (cog shapes are shown by default) in the window.

4. Click a style thumbnail to apply it to the selected object(s).

To remove an object style from a gallery:

- Right-click the thumbnail and choose **Delete**.

To unlink an object from its style definition:

- Right-click the object and choose **Format>Object Style>Unlink**.

If you've applied a style to an object but have lost track of the thumbnail—or want to confirm which style is actually being used on an object—you can quickly locate the thumbnail from the object.

To locate an object's style in the Styles tab:

- Right-click the object and choose **Format>Object Style>Locate in Studio**.

The Styles tab displays the gallery thumbnail for the object's style.

Normally, a publication's object styles are just stored locally—that is, as part of that publication; they don't automatically carry over to new publications. If you've created a new style you'll want to use in another publication, you can save it globally so that it will appear in the Styles tab each time you open a new publication.

Saving Object Styles

To create a new object style based on an existing object's attributes:

1. Right-click the object and choose **Format>Object Style>Create**.

    The Style Attributes Editor dialog appears, with a tree listing object attributes on the left and a preview region on the right (not shown).

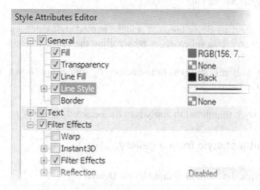

2. Click to expand or collapse sections within the attributes tree. Check any attributes you want to include in the style definition, and uncheck any you don't want to include.

3. If you want to change any of the current object settings, double-click an attribute (or select it and click the **Edit** button). This will bring up a detailed dialog for the particular attribute.

4. The **Object** pane in the preview region shows the currently selected object after applying the defined style. Select the **Artistic Text** or **Frame Text** tab to see the style applied to sample objects of those types.

5. Click the **Browse...** button to select the gallery category where you want to locate the style thumbnail, and optionally, save to a different Preview Type (Rounded Rectangle, Frame Text, or Artistic Text) instead of the default cog shape.

6. Type a name to identify the gallery thumbnail.

7. Click **OK**. A thumbnail for the new object style appears in the designated gallery.

Once an object style is listed in a gallery, you can modify it or create a copy (for example, to define a derivative style) by right-clicking on its thumbnail and choosing **Edit...** or **Copy...**.

To save a publication's object styles globally:

1. Choose **Save Defaults...** from the **Tools** menu.

2. From the dialog, check **Object styles**, then click **Save**.

Using the Gallery

The **Gallery tab** serves as a container for storing your own design objects you'd like to reuse in different publications. It also includes sample designs and is stocked with a wide variety of pre-designed elements that you can customize and use as a starting point for your own designs. Once you've copied a design to the Gallery, it becomes available in any publication—simply open the Gallery!

Designs are stored in categories such as Business, Education, Fun, Picture Frames, Logos, and Flashes.

The Gallery has two parts: an upper **Categories** drop-down menu and a lower **Designs** window showing a list of thumbnails representing the designs in the selected category. You can adopt a design by dragging the thumbnail onto the page.

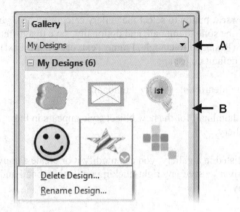

(A) Categories,(B)Designs

The Gallery tab can store your own designs in the ready-to-go **My Designs** category—the design is made available in any PagePlus project. When you first install PagePlus, the My Designs gallery will be empty, ready for custom designs to be added to it. New categories can be created at any time.

To further arrange your designs into logical groupings, you can add sub-categories to My Designs or to any other custom or pre-defined category.

🔖 Designs can be added to any pre-supplied category; the My Designs category exists simply for ease of use when storing your own custom designs.

To use a design from the Gallery:

- Click its thumbnail in the design category and drag it out onto the page. The Gallery retains a copy of the design until you expressly delete it.

To view your Gallery:

1. Click the Studio's **Gallery** tab.

2. Select a category from the drop-down menu. The items from the first listed subcategory are displayed by default.

To add, delete, or rename custom categories:

1. With the Gallery tab selected, click ▷ **Tab Menu** and choose **Add category...**, **Remove category**, or **Rename category...** from the drop-down list.

2. Use the dialog to enter and/or confirm your change.

If adding a category, you need to name the category in a dialog. For removal or deletion, simply pick the category in advance of picking the option.

> All designs in a deleted category will also be lost!

To add, delete, or rename custom sub categories:

- To add, select a category and click **Add Sub Category...** from the tab's ▷ **Tab Menu** button.

- To delete or rename, select options from the ⬇ drop-down button on the sub category title bar.

To move or copy an object into the Gallery:

1. Using the Categories drop-down menu, select a category into which you want to add the object. Scroll to reveal target sub-categories, expanding them if necessary.

2. Drag the object from the page and drop it onto the target category or sub-category design window (drag onto an empty sub-categories title bar to add). To copy, press the **Ctrl** key before starting to drag. A thumbnail of the design appears in the Designs window.

To rename or delete a custom design from the Gallery:

- Click on the ⬇ drop-down button in the bottom-right corner of a thumbnail (shown by hover over) and choose from the menu.

Using connectors

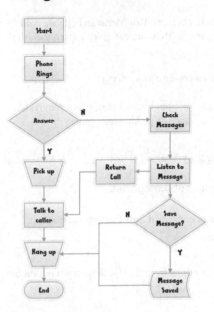

Two Connector tools let you create dynamic link lines between any two objects. These connectors remain anchored to the objects, even if either or both of them are moved or resized. So, for example, it's easy to create a flow chart with connectors between boxes, then freely rearrange the layout while preserving the directional relationships!

As connectors are treated as ordinary lines, you can colour them (see p. 225) and format them with the Line tab to add arrows, feathers, or other decorative line end. (See Setting line properties on p. 199.)

Connector types

- The **Connector Tool** lets you draw a single, straight-line connector between any two connection points.

- The **Elbow Connector Tool** lets you draw a connector with only vertical and horizontal segments—for example, if you're creating a flow chart, organization chart, or tree diagram.

Connection points

To make connections easy, each object has default square connection points, displayed whenever you select a Connector tool and hover over a target object.

These default points (which can't be moved or deleted) are normally evenly distributed around an object's shape.

To create a connector:

1. For a straight-line connector, select the **Connector Tool** on the Connector Tools flyout (**Tools** toolbar).

    - or -

    For an elbow connector, select the **Elbow Connector Tool**.

2. Hover over an object so that default **connection points** become visible.

3. Drag from the object's connection point to another object's connection point. Release the mouse button when the pointer is over the target connection point. A direct connector will appear between the two connection points.

Instead of using an object's default connection points, you can create your own custom connection points by:

- hovering over any shape's edge and dragging from that red originating point.

    - or -

- creating a custom connection point with the Connection Point Tool.

They can also be placed anywhere on the page, and are especially useful when creating a connection onto grouped QuickShapes or more complex grouped objects such as symbols.

To add a custom connection point (with Connection Point Tool):

1. Select an object.

2. Select the ⊠ **Connection Point Tool** on the Connector Tools flyout (**Tools** toolbar).

3. Click at a chosen location to place the custom connection point (inside or outside the object). The custom connection point appears in blue.

To view the connection points again you have to hover over the object which was selected while the connection point was created. Remember to enable either the Connector Tool or Elbow Connector Tool in advance.

Editing connection points and connectors

*   ⊠ To move a custom connection point, select the object to which it is associated and drag the point with the **Connection Point Tool**.

*   ⊠ To delete a custom connection point you've added, use the **Connection Point Tool** to click the object to which the connection point was associated, click the connection point you want to delete, and then press Delete. Default nodes are fixed and can't be deleted.

*   ▶ To move, reshape, or detach/reattach a connector, use the **Pointer Tool** to drag individual nodes. Drag the end node of a connector to detach or reattach it. (See Drawing and editing lines on p. 196).

7 Colour, Fills, and Transparency

Applying solid fills

PagePlus offers a number of ways to apply solid colour fills to objects of different kinds:

- You can apply solid colours to an object's **line** or **fill**. As you might expect, QuickShapes and closed shapes (see Drawing and editing shapes on p. 201) have both line and fill properties, whereas straight and freehand lines have only a line property.

- Characters in text objects can have fill colour or highlight colour. Text frames and table cells can have a background fill independent of the characters they contain.

- You can colourize a paint-type (bitmap) picture—that is, recolour it to use a different colour. If you recolour a full-colour picture, the colours will convert to tints or shades of the specified colour. You can also apply tinting to a full-colour picture to produce a low-intensity picture (useful for backgrounds behind text).

You can use the Colour tab, Swatches tab or a dialog box to apply solid colours to an object.

To apply a solid colour via the Colour tab:

1. Select the object(s) or highlight a range of text.

2. Click the **Colour** tab and select one of several colour modes (RGB, CMYK, or HSL) from the drop-down list.

3. Click the ⬒ **Fill**, ▬ **Line**, or **A** **Text** button at the top of the tab to determine where colour will be applied. The colour of the underline reflects the colour of your selected object. For selected frame text, the Fill will be the background text colour (but not the frame's background colour).

4. Select a colour from the colour spectrum or sliders depending on colour mode selected.

To apply a solid colour via the Swatches tab:

1. Select the object(s) or highlight a range of text.

2. Click the **Swatches** tab.

3. Click the 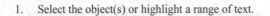 **Fill**, **Line**, or **A Text** button at the top of the tab to determine where colour will be applied.

4.  Select a colour swatch from the **Publication palette** (commonly used colours and those previously applied to your publication) or standard **Palette** (supplied preset swatches).

Alternatively, use **Format>Fill...** to apply colour via a dialog.

To change a solid colour's shade/tint (lightness):

1. Select the object and set the correct Fill, Line or Text button in the Colour tab.

2. From the Colour mode drop-down menu, select **Tinting**.

3. Drag the Shade/Tint slider to the left or right to darken or lighten your starting colour, respectively. You can also enter a percentage value in the box (entering 0 in the input box reverts to the original colour).

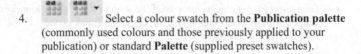 Adjust the `0%` percentage tinting via slider or direct input to apply object tinting from the Swatches tab.

PagePlus automatically adds used colours to the 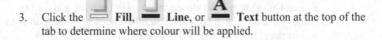 **Publication Palette** in the Swatches tab.

To change the current palette:

- Click the 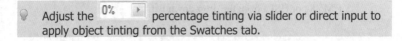 **Palette** button to view and adopt colours from a **Standard RGB**, **Standard CMYK**, or selection of themed palettes. Colours can be added, edited, or deleted from the Publication Palette but not from other palettes.

Using colour schemes

In PagePlus, a **colour scheme** is a cluster of five complementary colours that you can apply to specific elements in one or more publications. The **Schemes** tab displays preset schemes which can be selected at any point during the design process.

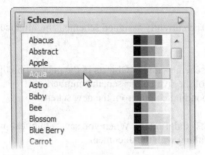

Each publication can have just one colour scheme at a time; the current scheme is highlighted in the **Schemes** tab. You can easily switch schemes, modify scheme colours and create custom schemes. Colour schemes are saved globally, so the full set of schemes is always available.

How colour schemes work

Colour schemes in PagePlus work much like a paint-by-numbers system, where various regions of a layout are coded with numbers, and a specific colour is assigned (by number) to each region. For example, imagine a line drawing coded with the numbers 1 through 5. To fill it in, you'd use paint from jars also numbered 1 through 5. Swapping different colours into the paint jars, while keeping the numbers on the drawing the same, would produce quite a different painting.

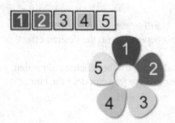

In PagePlus, the "paint jars" are five numbers you can assign to objects in your publication. They're known as "Scheme Colour 1," "Scheme Colour 2," and so on. When you apply Scheme Colour 1 to an object, it's like saying, "Put the colour from jar number 1 here."

- The **Schemes** tab shows the various available schemes, each with a different set of five colours in the five "jars." Whichever named colour scheme you select, that scheme's first colour (as shown in its sample) will appear in regions defined as Scheme Colour 1, its second colour will map to Scheme Colour 2, and so on throughout the publication.

To select a colour scheme:

1. Click the Schemes tab. The currently assigned scheme is highlighted in the list.

2. Click a different colour scheme sample. Objects in the publication that have been assigned one of the five colour scheme numbers are updated with the corresponding colour from the new scheme.

You can repeat this selection process indefinitely. When you save a publication, its current colour scheme is saved along with the document.

Applying scheme colours to objects

When you create publications from pre-defined design templates (see p. 20), you can choose the starting colour scheme that you want to adopt; you can always change it later from the Schemes tab. This flexibility creates endless possibilities for the look and feel of your publication! However, if you then create new elements in your schemed publication, or start a publication from scratch, how can you extend the current colour scheme to the new objects? Although you'll need to spend some time working out which colour combinations look best, the mechanics of the process are simple. Recalling the paint-by-numbers example above, all you need to do is assign one of the five current scheme colour numbers to an object's line and/or fill.

To assign a scheme colour to an object:

1. Select the object and choose a ⬒ **Fill**, ▬ **Line**, or **A** **Text** button at the top of the Swatches tab depending on the desired effect.

2. From the bottom of the Swatches tab, click on the scheme colour that you want to apply to the fill, line, or text (or you can drag the colour instead).

If an object's fill uses a scheme colour, the corresponding sample in Swatches tab will be highlighted whenever the object is selected.

PagePlus lets you create your own scheme by modifying an existing colour scheme in **Colour Scheme Designer** or by creating your scheme from scratch. See PagePlus Help for more information.

Creating custom colour schemes

If you've tried various preset colour schemes but haven't found one that's quite right, you can use the **Colour Scheme Designer** to modify any of the colours in an existing scheme (to create a new one) or create your own named scheme from scratch.

Modifying existing colour schemes

To modify a colour scheme:

1. From the Schemes tab, select a colour scheme to be modified from the list.

2. Select **Colour Scheme Designer...** from the **Tools** menu.
   - or -
   Click on the Schemes tab's ▷ **Tab Menu** button and choose **Colour Scheme Designer...** from the drop-down menu.

   The **Colour Scheme Designer** dialog appears.

3. From the **Colour Scheme** list at the right of your dialog, each of the five scheme colour numbers has its own drop-down list, showing available colours in the PagePlus palette.
   Click the down arrow on the scheme colour you want to modify.
   (Additionally, you'll see options for web publishing scheme colours for Hyperlink, Followed Hyperlink, Active Hyperlink, Rollover Hyperlink, Background and On-page.)

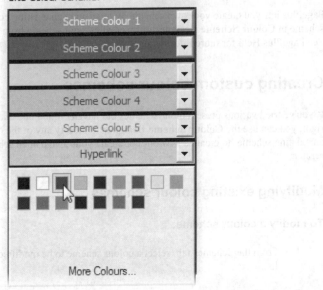

Site Colour Scheme:

4. Select a new colour from the palette or from the Colour Selector (click **More Colours...**).

5. Click **OK**. This saves the scheme locally (i.e., just for the publication) and shows in the Swatches tab for easy colour assignment.

> To store the modified scheme under a new scheme name in the Schemes tab, jump to the dialog's **Colour Scheme** tab and click **Save As**. Alternatively, the **Save** option just overwrites the preset. Both options make the new scheme global (available to all new publications).

Creating custom schemes from colour spreads

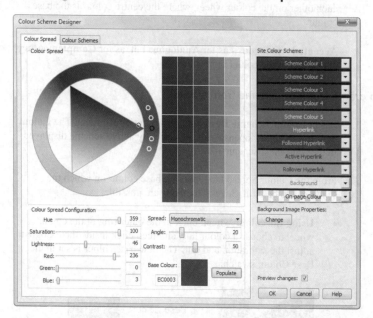

The Colour Scheme Designer lets you create eye-catching custom colour schemes from colour spreads.

To start, you choose a **base colour** on which to build your scheme, then you pick from a selection of **colour spreads**—grids of colours based on established colour theory models. Each spread suggests different colour choices for your scheme.

- **Monochromatic** (shown above) - derived from variations of lightness and saturation on the chosen base colour.

- **Complementary** - derived from variations of the base colour and of the colour that sits opposite it on the colour wheel.

- **Triadic** - derived from variations of three colours (one of which is the base colour), spaced equally around the colour wheel.

- **Tetradic** - derived from variations of four colours, arranged around the colour wheel in two complementary colour pairs.

- **Analogous** - derived from variations of colours that are adjacent to each other on the colour wheel, where the centre colour is the base colour.

- **Accented Analogous** - as for **Analogous** but, as for **Complementary**, also includes the colour opposite.

To create a colour scheme from scratch:

1. Select **Colour Scheme Designer...** from the **Tools** menu. The **Colour Scheme Designer** opens, with the currently active scheme displayed in the right-hand scheme list.

2. From the Colour Spread tab, choose a base colour on which the scheme is to be built. Several methods are possible:

   - **Using the colour wheel**: click in the outer ring of the colour wheel to choose a colour hue, and then click inside the triangle to adjust the saturation and tint. The new base colour is set in the Base Colour swatch.

   The base colour is the colour directly under the marker that sits inside the colour wheel's triangle.

   - **Entering HSL or RGB values**: use the sliders or input boxes to specify a base colour exactly.

   - **Drag-and-drop**: drag a colour from the Colour Scheme list onto the colour wheel (or base colour swatch).

   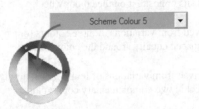

With any method, the base colour updates to show the new colour.

3. Select a colour spread type from the **Spread** drop-down list.

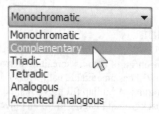

The colour spread, a grid of suggested colours, updates according to the chosen spread type. The spread offers a range of suggested colours to choose from. The number of colours presented may differ with the spread type.

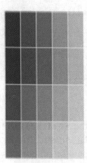

4. (Optional) Use the **Angle** and/or **Contrast** slider to modify the spread.

5. Once you're happy with the spread colours offered, you can create your scheme either via:

    •   **one-click**: click the **Populate** button next to the Base colour swatch. The site colour scheme is updated automatically with multiple colours.

    •   **colour-by-colour selection**: drag individual colour(s) from the grid onto a scheme colour on the Colour Scheme list.

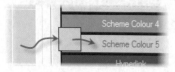

6. To apply the scheme, click **OK**. The colour scheme is now updated and stored in the publication.

To save the scheme globally so it can be used in other publications, jump to the Colour Schemes tab, then click **Save As...**.

Gradient and bitmap fills

Gradient fills provide a gradation or spectrum of colours spreading between two or more points on an object. A gradient fill has an editable path with nodes that mark the origin of each of these key colours. A bitmap fill uses a named bitmap—often a material, pattern, or background image—to fill an object.

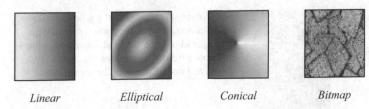

Linear   *Elliptical*   *Conical*   *Bitmap*

You can apply preset gradient and bitmap fills from the **Swatches tab** to the fill or outline of a shape or text frame; table cells as well as artistic, frame, and table text can also take a gradient or bitmap fill. The fill's path on an object's fill or line can also be varied for different effects (see PagePlus Help).

Vestibulum semper enim non eros. Sed vitae arcu. Aliquam erat volutpat. Praesent odio nisl, suscipit et rhoncus sit amet, porttitor sit amet, leo. Aenean hendrerit est. Etiam ac augue. Morbi tincidunt neque ut lacus. Donec ante cursus orci.

Applying a gradient or bitmap fill

There are several ways to apply a gradient or bitmap fill: using the Swatches **tab**, the **Fill Tool**, or a dialog.

The easiest way to apply a gradient or bitmap fill is to use one of a range of pre-supplied swatch thumbnails in the Swatches tab's **Gradient** or **Bitmap** palettes. The **Fill Tool** and a Fill dialog are alternative methods for creating gradient fills.

To apply a gradient or bitmap fill using the Swatches tab:

1. Display the Swatches tab and ensure either 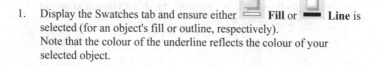 **Fill** or **▬ Line** is selected (for an object's fill or outline, respectively).
    Note that the colour of the underline reflects the colour of your selected object.

2. For gradient fills, select a gradient category, e.g. Linear, Elliptical, etc., from the **Gradient** button's drop-down menu.
    - or -

    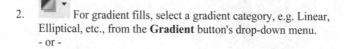 For bitmap fills, select a drop-down menu category from the **Bitmap** button.

3. Select the object(s), and then click the appropriate gallery swatch for the fill you want to apply.
    - or -

    For fills only, drag from the gallery swatch onto any object and release the mouse button.

4. If needed, adjust the fill's **Tint** at the bottom of the tab with the tab slider or set a percentage value in the input box.

🖎 Applying different transparency effects (using the **Transparency** tab) won't alter the object's fill settings as such, but may significantly alter a fill's actual appearance.

To apply a gradient fill with the Fill Tool:

1. Select an object.

2. Click the  **Fill Tool** button on the **Attributes** toolbar's Fill flyout.

3. Display the Swatches tab and ensure either  **Fill** or  **Line** is selected (for an object's fill or outline, respectively).

4. Click and drag on the object to define the fill path. The object takes a simple Linear fill, grading from the object's current colour to monochrome white.

> If the object is white already (or has no fill), grading is from white to black.

Alternatively, a dialog can be used to add or subtract **key colours** from the gradient, apply different key colours to individual nodes, or vary the overall shading of the effect applied to the object.

To apply or edit a gradient or bitmap fill using a dialog:

1. Display the Swatches tab and ensure either  **Fill** or  **Line** is selected (for an object's fill or outline, respectively).

2. Right-click the object and choose **Format>Fill**, or select it and choose **Fill...** from the **Format** menu.
   - or -

   Click the  **Edit Fill** button on the **Attributes** toolbar's Fill flyout.

3. Choose the fill type and the desired fill category. Note that you can also use the dialog to apply a solid fill.

- For gradient fills, select **Gradient** from the **Type** drop-down menu, and pick a gradient preset. A two-colour gradient has two nodes, one at each end of its path.
  - or -

  Click the **From** and **To** buttons to specify the gradient's start and end colours.
  - or -

  Click the **Edit** button if you want to add or subtract key colours from the currently chosen gradient, apply different key colours to individual nodes, or vary the overall shading of the effect.

- For bitmap fills, select **Bitmap** from the **Type** drop-down menu, choose a category, and then click a gallery swatch.

4. Click **OK** to apply the effect or fill to the object.

Editing the fill path

When you select a fillable object, the **Fill Tool** becomes available (otherwise it's greyed out). When you select the Fill Tool, if the object uses a **gradient fill**, you'll see the **fill path** displayed as a line, with nodes marking where the spectrum between each key colour begins and ends. Adjusting the node positions determines the actual spread of colours between nodes. You can also edit a gradient fill by adding, deleting, or changing key colours.

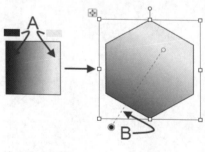

Linear Fill based   *Filled object*
on key colours (A)   *showing fill path*
                                  (B)

To adjust the gradient fill path on a selected object:

1. Display the Swatches tab and ensure either ⬜ **Fill** or ▬ **Line** is
   selected (for an object's fill or outline, respectively).

2. Click the ◇ **Fill Tool** button on the **Attributes** toolbar's Fill flyout.
   The fill path appears on the object's fill or outline.

3. Use the **Fill Tool** to drag the start and end path nodes, or click on the
   object for a new start node and drag out a new fill path. The gradient
   starts where you place the start node, and ends where you place the
   end node.

Each gradient fill type has a characteristic path. For example, Linear fills have
single-line paths, while Radial fills have a two-line path so you can adjust the
fill's extent in two directions away from the centre. If the object uses a **bitmap
fill**, you'll see the fill path displayed as two lines joined at a centre point. Nodes
mark the fill's centre and edges.

Working with transparency

Transparency effects are great for highlights, shading and shadows, and simulating "rendered" realism. They can make the critical difference between flat-looking publications and publications with depth and snap. PagePlus fully supports variable transparency and lets you apply solid, gradient, or bitmap transparencies to an object's fill or outline easily.

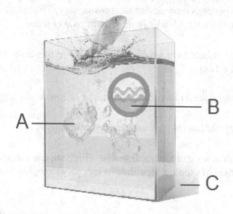

(A) bitmap transparency, (B) solid transparency, (C) gradient transparency

Transparencies work rather like fills that use "disappearing ink" instead of colour. The more transparency in a particular spot, the more "disappearing" takes place there, and the more the object(s) underneath show through. Just as a gradient fill can vary from light to dark, a transparency can vary from more to less, i.e. from clear to opaque, as in the illustration:

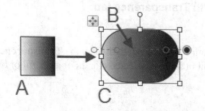

(A) Linear Transparency, (B) Path,(C) Effect on Object

In PagePlus, transparency effects work very much like greyscale fills. Just like fills...

- Transparency effects are applied from the Studio—in this case, using the **Transparency tab**. (Transparency is also an option with the 3D Pattern Map filter effect.)

- The Transparency tab's gallery has thumbnails in shades of grey, where the lighter portions represent more transparency. To apply transparency, you click thumbnails or drag them onto objects.

- Most transparency effects have a path you can edit—in this case, with the **Transparency Tool**.

Transparency types available in the Transparency tab are as follows:

- **Solid** transparency distributes the transparency uniformly.

- **Gradient** transparencies include linear, radial, elliptical, and conical effects (each thumbnail's tooltip identifies its category), ranging from clear to opaque.

- **Bitmap** transparencies include categorized texture maps based on the Swatches tab's selection of bitmaps.

Applying transparency

You can apply transparency to shapes, text frames, table cells, and to any artistic, frame, and table text.

To apply transparency with Transparency tab:

1. With your object selected, display the **Transparency tab** and ensure either **Fill** or **Line** is selected (for an object's fill or outline, respectively).

2. For solid transparency, select the **Solid** button and pick a thumbnail from the solid transparency gallery. The lighter thumbnails represent more transparency (expressed as percentage Opacity).
   - or -

For gradient transparency, choose the 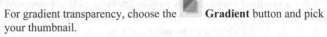 **Gradient** button and pick your thumbnail.

- or -

For bitmap transparency, choose the **Bitmap** button and pick a thumbnail from a range of categories.

3. The transparency is applied to the object's fill or outline.

Alternatively, drag the desired thumbnail from the gallery to an object, and release the mouse button.

To apply gradient transparency with the Transparency Tool:

1. Select the object and set the Transparency tab's **Fill/Line** swatch as before.

2. Click the **Transparency Tool** on the **Attributes** toolbar's Transparency flyout.
   - or -
   Select **Format>Transparency...**.

3. Drag your cursor across the object and release the mouse button. The object takes a simple Linear transparency, grading from 100% opacity to 0% opacity (fully transparent).

Editing transparency

Once you've applied a gradient transparency, you can adjust or replace its **path** on the object, and the **level** of transparency along the path. You can even create more complex transparency effects by adding extra nodes to the path by clicking and assigning different levels to each node.

To adjust the transparency path:

- Use the **Transparency Tool** to drag individual nodes, or click on the object for a new start node and drag out a new transparency path. The effect starts where you place the start node, and ends where you place the end node. For bitmap transparencies, the path determines the centre and two edges of the effect.

Editing a **gradient transparency** path is similar to editing a comparable fill path. Adding a level of transparency means varying the transparency gradient; this is done by introducing a new **node** and assigning it a particular value. For transparencies with multiple nodes, each node has its own value, comparable to a key colour in a gradient fill. Note that you cannot alter the values in a bitmap transparency.

To edit a gradient transparency directly:

1. Select the object and set the Transparency tab's **Fill/Line** swatch as before.

2. Click ![icon] **Transparency Tool** on the **Attributes** toolbar. The object's transparency path appears on the fill or line, with start and end nodes.

3. To **add** a transparency node, drag from any **solid transparency** sample in the Transparency tab to the point on the path where you want to add the node.

   The higher the percentage value assigned to a transparency node, the more transparent the effect at that point. Note: The hue of the colour doesn't matter, only its percentage value—so it's much easier just to choose from the set of gallery thumbnails.

4. To **change** the transparency value of any existing node, including the start and end nodes, select the node and click on a new thumbnail in the Transparency tab's Solid transparency gallery (you can also drag your chosen thumbnail onto the selected node)

5. To **move** a node you've added, simply drag it to a new position along the transparency path.

6. To **delete** a node you've added, select it and press **Delete**.

Setting the default transparency

The **default transparency** means the transparency that will be applied to the next new object you create. Local defaults only affect objects in the current project. For information on setting defaults in PagePlus, see Updating and saving defaults on p. 29.

8 Printing
your Publication

Printing basics

Printing your publication to a desktop printer is one of the more likely operations you'll be performing in PagePlus. The easy-to-use Print dialog presents the most commonly used options to you, with a navigable "live" Preview window to check your print output.

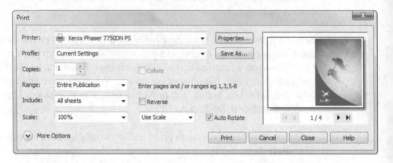

The dialog also supports additional printing options via the **More Options** button including **Double-sided Printing/Manual Duplex**, **Mail Merge**, **Rasterize**, and many other useful printing options. One particular option, called **Layout** (p. 249), allows for **print-time imposition** of your publication—simply create a booklet or other folder publication at the print stage.

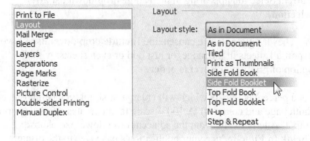

For a detailed description of each option, see Previewing the Printed Page in PagePlus Help.

Here we'll cover what you need to know for basic desktop printer output. If you're working with a service bureau or professional printer and need to provide professional PDF output, see Generating professional output in PagePlus Help.

To set up your printer or begin printing:

1. Click   **Print** on the **Standard** toolbar. The Print dialog appears.

2. Select a currently installed printer from the **Printer** drop-down list. If necessary, click the **Properties** button to set up the printer for the correct page size, etc.

3. Select a printer profile from the **Profile** drop-down list. You can just use **Current Settings** or choose a previously saved custom profile (.ppr) based on a combination of dialog settings; **Browse...** lets you navigate to any .ppr file on your computer. To save current settings, click the **Save As...** button, and provide a unique profile name. The profile is added to the drop-down list.

4. Select the number of copies to print, and optionally instruct the printer to **Collate** them.

5. Select the print **Range** to be printed, e.g. the Entire Publication, Current Page, or range of pages. For specific pages or a range of pages, enter "1,3,5" or "2-5", or enter any combination of the two.

   To print selected text or objects, make you selection first, then choose Current Selection appearing in the **Range** drop-down list **after selection**.

   Whichever option you've chosen, the **Include** drop-down list lets you export all sheets in the range, or just odd or even sheets, with the option of printing in **Reverse order**.

4. Set a percentage **Scale** which will enlarge or shrink your print output (both page and contents). A 100% scale factor creates a full size print output. Alternatively, from the adjacent drop-down list, choose **Shrink to Fit** to reduce your publication's page size to the printer sheet size or **Scale to Fit** to enlarge or reduce the publication page size as required.

5. Keep **Auto Rotate** checked if you want your publication page to automatically rotate your printer's currently set sheet orientation. When you access the Print dialog, if page and sheet sizes do not match, you'll be prompted to adjust your printer sheet orientation automatically (or you can just ignore auto-rotation).

6. Click **Print**.

More print options

Additional print options are available from the Print dialog if you're planning to use imposition at print time (see p. 249), use specific PagePlus features which use printing (e.g., Mail Merge), print double-sided, or generate professional output.

Interactive Print Preview

The **Print Preview** mode changes the screen view to display your layout without frames, guides, rulers, and other screen items. Supporting toolbars allow for a comprehensive and interactive preview of your publication pages before printing.

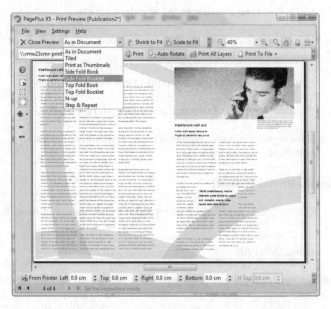

Print Preview is interactive because a main feature is to provide **print-time imposition**. Put simply, this allows you to create folded books, booklets, and more, **at the printing stage** from unfolded basic page setups. Other interactive features are also available while in Print Preview.

- Select installed printers, and choose which pages to print and how they print (to printer, file or separation).

- Add and adjust printer margins.

- Switch on/off page marks when generating professional output.

- Control which database records print when using mail and photo merge via a Mail and Photo Merge toolbar.

Don't forget to make the most of Print Preview's powerful **viewing controls** hosted on the **View** toolbar. Use zoom controls, Pan/Zoom tools, and multi-page views for detailed preview work.

To preview the printed page:

1. Click **Print Preview** on the **Standard** toolbar.

In Print Preview, your first printer sheet is displayed according to your printer's setup.

2. (Optional) Choose an installed printer from the **Printer** toolbar.

3. (Optional) Adjust printer margins from the **Margins** toolbar.

4. Review you publication using the page navigation controls at the bottom of your workspace.

To print via Printer toolbar:

1. Choose which page to print via the **Print Publication** drop-down list.

2. Select **Print**.

The standard Print dialog is then displayed, where settings are carried over from Print Preview.

To cancel Print Preview mode:

- Select ✕ **Close Preview** from the top of your workspace (or click the window's ✕ **Close** button).

Print-time imposition

During print preview, you can enable imposition of your document, choosing a mode suited to your intended printed document (book, booklet, etc.). Each mode displays different toolbar options on the context-sensitive **Imposition** toolbar.

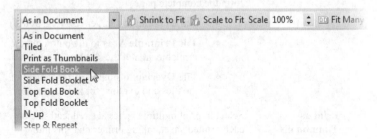

To choose an imposition mode:

- From the **Imposition** toolbar, select an option from the **Imposition Mode** drop-down list.

As in Document	Select to print pages as they appear in your document, i.e. one page per sheet. Scaling options include: • **Shrink to fit** to reduce the page to the printer sheet size. • **Scale to fit** to adjust artwork automatically to fit neatly on the printed page, taking printer margins into account. • **Scale** to specify a custom scaling percentage. The default is 100% or normal size. To scale your work to be printed at a larger size, specify a larger value; to scale down, specify a smaller value. • If you haven't set up the publication as a Small Publication, but still want to print multiple pages per sheet, try using the **Fit Many**. Note that this option ignores printer margins and doesn't change the imposition (orientation) of output pages. Ensure your page layout borders don't extend beyond the printable region.

Tiled	Even if the publication isn't set up as a **poster** or **banner**, you can use tiling and scaling settings to print onto multiple sheets from a standard size page. Each section or tile is printed on a single sheet of paper, and the various tiles can then be joined to form the complete page.
	• **Scale** to print at a larger size (e.g. 300%).
	• **Tile Printable Area** to tile onto only the printable area of the sheet.
	• **Tile Overlap** to simplify arrangement of the tiles and to allow for printer margins.
Print as Thumbnails	Select to print multiple pages at a reduced size on each printed sheet, taking printer margins into account.
	• Set the number of thumbnails per sheet in the **Per Sheet** box.
	PagePlus will print each page of the publication at a reduced size, with the specified number of small pages or "thumbnails" neatly positioned on each printed sheet.
Side Fold Book	Select to paginate as a side fold book, optionally using scaling options described above.
Side Fold Booklet	Select to paginate as a side fold booklet, optionally using scaling options described above.
Top Fold Book	Select to paginate as a top fold book, optionally using scaling options described above.
Top Fold Booklet	Select to paginate as a top fold booklet, optionally using scaling options described above.
N-up/N-up Repeat	Select to paginate with multiple pages on the printer sheet, with each page repeating a configurable number of times. Great for business cards and labels!
	• **Across** sets the number of copies across the page.
	• **Down** sets the number of copies down the page.

	• **Repeat** selects the number of times to repeat each page.
	• **Skip** lets you omit a certain number of regions on the first sheet of paper. Skipping regions is useful if, for example, you've already peeled off several labels from a label sheet, and don't want to print on the peeled-off sections.
	• **Fill Last Page** will populate the last page with your repeating region rather than just printing an almost blank page.
Step & Repeat	Select to paginate with multiple pages on the printer sheet, with each sheet containing copies of the same page only.
	• **Across** sets the number of copies across the page.
	• **Down** sets the number of copies down the page.

Printing books and booklets

To produce double-sided sheets, click 🖶 **Print** and use the Print dialog's Double-sided Printing or Manual Duplex options (under More Options). Ensure your printer is setup for double-sided printing or run sheets through twice, printing first the front and then the back of the sheet (reverse top and bottom between runs). The sheets can then be collated and bound at their centre to produce a booklet, with all the pages in the correct sequence.

Working in Trimmed Page Mode

Trimmed Page Mode is similar to Print Preview mode but lets you toggle between the page you're currently working on (complete with visible guides, pasteboard objects, text marks, special l characters, etc.) and a preview page which shows how your page will appear in print. You can still edit page content while in Trimmed Page mode.

To enter Trimmed Page mode:

- Click ⊡ **Trimmed Page Mode** on the **Hintline** toolbar.

9 Publishing and Sharing

Exporting PDF files

PDF (short for Portable Document Format) is a cross-platform WYSIWYG file format developed by Adobe to handle documents in a device- and platform-independent manner. The format has evolved into a worldwide standard for document distribution which works equally well for online or professional electronic publishing.

To export your publication as a PDF file:

1. Prepare the publication following standard print publishing guidelines, and taking the distribution method into account.

2. (Optional) Insert hyperlinks as needed, for example to link table of contents entries to pages in the document.

3. (Optional) To create **pop-up annotations**, insert PageHints as needed.

4. (Optional) Once the publication is final, prepare a bookmark list (see Creating a PDF bookmark list on p. 256).
   Note: Bookmarks appear as a separate list in a special pane when the PDF file is viewed. They can link to a specific page or to an **anchor** (for example, a piece of text or a graphic object) in your publication.

5. Click 📄 **Publish PDF** on the **Standard** toolbar.

6. From the dialog, check your export settings. For a detailed explanation of each export setting see PagePlus Help.

7. Click **OK** to proceed to export.

If you checked **Preview PDF file** (General tab), the resulting PDF file appears in the version of Adobe Reader installed on your system.

Creating a PDF bookmark list

Bookmarks are optional links that appear in a separate pane of the Adobe Reader when a PDF file is displayed.

Typically, a bookmark links to a specific location such as a section heading in the publication, but it can also link to a whole page or specifically to an anchor attached to an object. You can insert bookmarks by hand, or PagePlus can apply **automatic generation** to produce a nested bookmark list up to six levels deep, derived from named styles in your publication.

You'll be able to view all your bookmarks at a glance, organize them, and create, modify or delete existing bookmarks as needed.

To use styles to automatically generate bookmarks:

1. Select **PDF Bookmarks...** from the **Insert** menu.

2. In the dialog, click **Automatic...**. You'll see a list of all the style names used in your publication. Check boxes to include text of a given style as a heading at a particular level (1 through 6).

Style	1st	2nd	3rd	4th	5th	6th
Footer	☐	☐	☐	☐	☐	☐
Header	☐	☐	☐	☐	☐	☐
Header an...	☐	☐	☐	☐	☐	☐
Heading	☐	☐	☐	☐	☐	☐
Heading 1	☒	☐	☐	☐	☐	☐
Heading 2	☐	☒	☐	☐	☐	☐
Heading 3	☐	☐	☒	☐	☐	☐
Heading 4	☐	☐	☐	☐	☐	☐

    To remove all bookmarks in the list, clear all check boxes.

3. Click **OK** to generate bookmarks.

The mechanics of **creating a PDF bookmark list by hand** are simple. For example, bookmarking a specific location (for example, a piece of text or a graphic object) entails placing an **anchor** at that location; the anchor serves as the target for the bookmark link.

To insert bookmarks by hand:

1. Select **PDF Bookmarks...** from the **Insert** menu.

2. In the bookmark tree, display the entry below which you want to create the new bookmark. (Check **Create as sub-entry** if you want the new bookmark nested as a "child" of the selected entry.)

3. Click the **Create...** button.

4. In the Create Bookmark dialog, enter the text for your bookmark in the **Bookmark Title** field. This text will be displayed in Adobe Reader as the bookmark name.

5. Click to select the bookmark destination type, then enter the destination.

   - To bookmark a specific page in the publication, set **Destination Type** to be **Page**, then select the target page's **Page Number**.

   - To bookmark to a specific location, set **Destination Type** to be **Anchor**, then select the target anchor's **Anchor Name**.

6. Click **OK** to confirm your choices.

You'll need to have created an anchor in advance to allow it to be bookmarked. You can create PDF bookmarks automatically when creating anchors. (See Adding anchors to objects on p. 83.)

To delete bookmarks:

1. Select **PDF Bookmarks...** from the **Insert** menu.

2. In the bookmark tree, select an entry for deletion, then click the **Remove** button. You'll be asked if you want to remove unused anchors.

A bookmark, if using an anchor, is also be deleted when the anchor is deleted (via **Insert>Anchor...**).

Unlike hyperlinks, bookmarks also work as actual links within PagePlus publications. You can use the bookmark list as a jumping-off point to any bookmarked entry.

Creating a PDF slideshow

The creation of PDF slideshows takes PagePlus's PDF publishing a step further. While a PDF file shows the exact replication of your original project for electronic distribution or printing, the PDF slideshow feature does the same, but with the intention of creating automated multimedia presentations. These can be shared by email and viewed without the need for special presentation software.

The main features of PDF slideshow include:

- Advance of each slide manually or automatically.

- Creation of multi-section slides from individual PagePlus pages.

- Use of slide-specific layer control (switch layers on or off).

- Freedom to reorder your slideshow.

- Apply slide-specific transition effects.

- Control of slide duration.

- Play a soundtrack for single slides or for the entire slideshow.

To publish a slideshow:

1. Select **Publish as PDF Slideshow...** from the **File** menu.

2. In the dialog, on the **General** tab, choose a default **Transition** type for all slides, e.g. Blinds, Wipe, or Dissolve. An individual slide can override this setting with its own transition setting.

3. Check **Manual Advance** if you don't want your slideshow to display slides one by one automatically—slides will be progressed manually by mouse-click or by pressing the space bar. For automatic slideshows, choose a **Duration**, i.e. the number of seconds each slide will remain on screen.

4. Uncheck **Preview PDF file** if you don't want to see a slideshow preview in your PDF reader immediately after publishing.

5. When your slideshow reaches the last page you can **Loop slideshow** continuously or **Return to normal view** to exit the slideshow.

6. In the **Compatibility** field, select a version of Adobe Reader for your intended audience.

7. For accompanying music, in the **Media** box, click the **Open** button to navigate to and select an audio file (WAV, MP3 and AIFF files).

8. Set a percentage **Scale**.

9. Select from the **Publish profile** drop-down list to choose a preset publishing profile. You can modify a selected profile to create custom profile settings using **Save As...**.

10. For multi-section slides, from the **Slides** tab, duplicate or copy a selected slide with the **Insert** or **Copy** button, respectively. Delete a slide if needed, or rearrange the playback order of existing slides with the **Up** or **Down** buttons. For more information, see Multi-section slides (see p. 260).

11. The Compression, Security and Advanced tabs are as described in Exporting PDF files (see p. 255), and should be set accordingly.

12. Click **OK**. In the dialog, save your named PDF file to a chosen location. If **Preview PDF file in Acrobat** was checked, your slideshow will start to run automatically.

Multi-section slides

One strength of the slideshow feature comes from the ability to make "multi-section" slide variants based on a single PagePlus page (this is done using page layers). Multi-section slides allow you to build up an image in sections; display multiple images and text objects sequentially on the same page; show and hide page elements; and so on. Simply create slides based on the original page then edit them by switching on/off specific layers to create unique slides. A few examples...

- Create time-delayed bulleted lists—great for mouse- or pointer-driven presentations.

- Introduce artistic elements to your page over time.

- Change photos over time.

To create multi-section slides:

1. In the **Slides** tab of the **Publish PDF Slideshow** dialog, choose a page from which you want to create a slide and click the **Insert** or **Copy** button. The former inserts a chosen slide above the currently selected slide as a copy; the latter simply places a copy above a selected slide.

2. Select the new slide and click the **Properties** button.

3. Set a slide-specific **Transition** and **Duration** (in seconds) from the drop-down menus.

4. Uncheck any layers which you don't want to be part of the slide to make it distinct from other slides.

5. Click the [...] browse button and then browse to and select a **Media** file, which will play while the slide is displayed. For the slide's duration, this will override any default media file set up to play throughout your slideshow.

6. Repeat the insert, copy, and layer control for another slide, building up your multi-section slide arrangement.

To undo the slide properties settings (reset the content of your slideshow so that there is only one slide per page), click the **Reset** button on the **Slides** tab.

Sharing by email

PagePlus lets you share publications as native PagePlus publications (.ppp) or as HTML, as a file attachment or as HTML within the body of your email, respectively.

Sharing PagePlus publications

1. With your publication open and in the currently active window, select **Send...** from the **File** menu.

   If you have multiple email programs and they are not loaded, a Choose Profile dialog lets you select your email program of choice, then a new email message is displayed with document attached. If already loaded, your email program automatically attaches your publication to a new email message.

2. Add the recipient's valid email address to the **To...** field (or equivalent).

3. Select the **Send** button (or equivalent) on your email program as for any other email message.

An Internet connection is required for the emailing of publications.

Sharing PagePlus publications as HTML or images

Interested in sharing content with recipients who may not be using PagePlus?
Send page as HTML lets you dispatch any page as HTML or as a bitmap. For
HTML, all referenced images and hyperlinks are embedded locally with the
message. For sharing as a bitmap, the message will be larger but will guarantee
that the document will appear as intended (great for ensuring compatibility with
older email clients).

Normally, an installed email client such as Outlook will be used by default.
However, if you don't have an installed email program or have Office (but don't
want to use it), you can use PagePlus to act as an email client instead. The only
prerequisite is having an outgoing SMTP mail server to transfer the email to—
you'll need to know the server address in advance.

To use PagePlus as an alternative email client:

- Select **Tools>Options...**, then select **Import settings**.

- Enable **Send HTML E-mail using PagePlus**, and enter the mail
  server name (e.g., mail-srv or mail.company.com). The port number
  25 is always used.

To share a document as an HTML page:

1. With your publication open, select the page you would like to send.

2. Select **Send Page as HTML...** from the **File** menu. The page is added
   to the body of a newly created HTML-based email message.

3. Add the recipient's valid email address to the **To...** field (or
   equivalent).

4. Select the **Send** button (or equivalent) on your email program.

To share a document as an image:

1. Check **Send entire HTML page as single image** in
   Tools>Options>HTML E-mail (in PagePlus).

2. Carry out procedure as for sharing a document as HTML above.

10 Using PDF Forms

Getting started with PDF forms

PagePlus lets you use electronic-based PDF forms to collect inputted data from readers of your publication in an efficient and modern manner. In much the same way as traditional paper forms are used to collect information (remember your last Tax Return!), PDF forms offer the same form completion concepts, but increase the interaction between publisher and audience by using an electronic medium.

Some common form types include Application forms, Contact Information forms, Request forms, Feedback forms, and Guest books.

One thing in common with all PDF forms is that they have to be published as PDF to operate. A PagePlus .ppp file with form functionality must be converted to PDF with **Publish PDF** (**Standard** toolbar).

Form Structure

The building blocks of a form comprise a mixture of text, graphics and **Form fields**. Form fields collect recipient data and can be added, moved and modified in a similar way to more familiar objects in PagePlus such as graphics and table elements. A field can be a Text field, Radio Button, Combo box, List box, Check box or a simple button.

Email Form

Name

E-mail Address

Comments

| Submit | Reset |

From the form recipient's perspective, information is typed into text boxes or selected from check boxes, radio buttons, or drop-down boxes. The information entered can be numeric, textual, or a mixture of both. It is possible to arrange and lock form fields, plus control the order in which form fields can be navigated (see Designing your PDF forms in PagePlus Help).

Each field has its own set of **Form Field Properties** relating to its appearance, its value(s), validation, calculations, and the action expected of the field.

In PagePlus, the form should be integrated into your Page design as you develop your publication. The form's functionality only then becomes active when a PDF of the form is generated. When a form recipient enters data into form fields the data can be collected as described below.

JavaScript is used to allow interactivity in your PDF forms. It drives formatting, validation, calculations, and actions—all key functions in PDF form development.

How is data collected?

Several methods exist for collecting forms once they have been completed.

- By Hardcopy **Print.**

- You can **Save Data to e-mail** (alternatively you can save data within the form).

- You can **Submit Data to Web** (a CGI application; by submission to a web-enabled server/database).

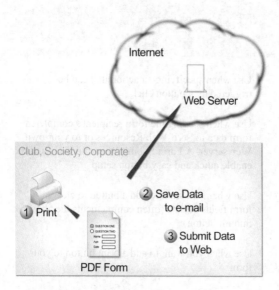

Creating PDF forms

Adding form fields

A series of form fields can be added to the page, depending on the type of form you want to create. Typically a mix of form fields will make up your finished form design.

Fields are created from the Form toolbar or via **Insert>Form Field**. You assign an internal unique name to each field and then set a variety of properties. Each form field has its own set of Form Field Properties which can be modified to suit your form implementation.

> The Form toolbar is turned off by default. Display it by going to **View>Toolbars>Form**.

Icon	Form Field Name	When to use?
OK	Button*	Use when specifying an action that can be triggered by a button click.
	Submit button*	Use when sending the form recipient's completed form data to Serif Web Resources or to your own Web server. A Form Submit Wizard is activated to enable quick and easy button setup.
	Reset button*	Use when you want to add a button to clear all form fields of data (often complements the above Submit button).
	Print button*	Use when you want to add a print button to your form.
☒	Check Box	Ideal when you want to multiply select a series of options displayed side by side. A good alternative to a Combo Box or List box if space allows.
I	Text Field	Use for adding text, numbers or a mixture of both.
▾	Combo Box	For selection from a scrollable list of items in a drop-down menu where only one item can be selected. The box also allows data entry to be input into this box type. Smaller than a List Box.
	List Box	For selection from a scrollable list of items; supports multiple selection and advanced actions on selection of menu items.
⦿	Radio Button	Good for selection of a single mutually exclusive item from a grouped subset of choices.
	Signature	Used for the digital signing of secure documents. See PagePlus Help.

* This button shares a drop down menu with other buttons marked with an asterisk. The button type previously chosen will always be displayed on the Form toolbar.

Form field properties

Form field properties control how the form field will operate when the form recipient enters their input. A series of tabs are arranged so that some tabs, e.g. **General**, **Appearance**, **Options**, or **Actions**, are common to all the form fields but others, such as **Format**, **Validation** and **Calculations** are only displayed for text fields and combo boxes.

To access Form Field Properties:

1. To view the properties do one of the following:

    - Right-click on a selected form field and choose **Form Field Properties**.

    - Double-click the form field.

    - Select the form field, and click the ⊙▤ button from the **Form** toolbar.

2. Click on one of several tabs for editing: General, Appearance, Options, Actions, Validate, or Calculate.

3. Click the **OK** or **Cancel** button to exit the dialog.

Publishing your PDF Form

- Click 📄 **Publish PDF** on the **Standard** toolbar.

See Exporting PDF files on p. 255 for more information.

> If you Publish as PDF using PDF/X-1 or PDF/X-1a compatibility, any PDF form fields present will be converted to graphics and will not be available. Choose an Acrobat option instead.

Collecting data from forms

Via hardcopy printout

This is a simple fill-in and print to hardcopy solution. This is great if your form recipients are located together, perhaps in the same office.

> ✎ If using Adobe® Reader®, any completed form data will be lost when you close your completed PDF form. Exceptions exist when using Standard or Professional software.

Within the PDF file

Alternatively, it is possible to store form data within the PDF Form itself by using the **Save** or **Save As...** command. One condition of this is that the form recipient must be using one of the following versions of Acrobat software:

- Adobe® Acrobat® 6.0 (or later) Standard or Professional.

- Adobe® Acrobat® 7.0 (or later) Elements.

> ✎ Adobe® Reader® software (6.0 and above) is unable to save form data within the form.

Using email

If you can save data within the PDF form then it's clear that you can email the completed form to the form originator. With the completed form still open, use **File>E-mail** to send the email to the intended recipient.

Via the web

Your PDF Form can be configured to be web ready by passing completed form data to a CGI application on a web server. This would typically be a server-sided web page designed to process the data and pass it to either a text file, database or other storage location. As an example, new subscriber details, collected via a PDF Form, can be sent automatically to a previously configured "subscribers" database.

All web-ready forms have one thing in common—they must be submitted to allow data to be collected. Typically, you may have come across this on web sites when you enter details into a form then submit the data by pressing a Submit button. The same applies for PDF forms—a **Submit** button can be configured in order to submit the form data to the web server. You can either create the button unaided or use the **Form Submit Wizard** (see below). Either way, the use of the submit process is the major difference between web-ready and other less dynamic forms.

The web process, as mentioned, requires a web server to operate. Not everyone will have access to or even want to operate their own web server so, as an alternative to this, you can use **Serif Web Resources**. This is a free web to email gateway service which will collect your valued form data at Serif and send it to your email address—the service does require that you firstly have a Customer login (for security reasons), which will allow you to create, edit and delete Form IDs via a web page accessible from the Wizard. The Form ID, a unique 30-digit number, is required for the service to operate and is generated automatically when you enter your destination email address in the above web page.

> ✒ No personal data will be stored on Serif web servers. All form data is redirected in real time.

Submitting Form Data

The submission of form data sounds a very complicated operation but by using a Form Submit Wizard the process is relatively straightforward. The Wizard not only creates a Submit button for your form, but configures the underlying submit process and the format in which your form data is to be stored in.

The submit process is made either to Serif Web Resources or to your own web server address (e.g., http://testserver.global.com/forms/collect.asp).

To run the Form Submit Wizard:

1. Select the ⌐⅃ **Submit Button** from the Button flyout menu on the **Form** toolbar.

2. In the first step, start the wizard by clicking the **Next>** button.

3. Choose either Serif Web Resources or your own server as the destination of your form recipient's data. The former is appropriate if you don't have access to your own web server.

1. **For Serif Web Resources**, click **Next>**.

2. Click the **Get a Form ID** button to display Serif's customer login web page. This page is where you log onto your customer account to enter firstly your email address to send form data to, and secondly to generate a unique Form ID for use in the secure email communication.

3. At the web page, if you already have a customer login you can enter your email address and password. For new customer you must register before continuing.

4. After login, select the **add form** link to enter the email address that you want your form data to be sent to.

5. Click the **Add Form** button. This generates an entry in the displayed list from which a 30-digit Form ID can be copied.

6. Paste the Form ID directly from the web page into the input field in your Wizard dialog.

7. Click the **Next>** button.

8. Select a Data format from the drop-down menu that you would like to store and transport your form data. Select one of: HTML, FDF, or XFDF. See PagePlus Help for more details.

- or -

1. **For your own web server**, click **Next>**.

2. Add your Web Server address to the displayed field, click **Next>**.

3. Choose an HTML, FDF, PDF or XFDF data format for exporting the form data. Check if you server is able to this format.

4. Finish the Wizard process by clicking the **Finish** button.

5. Move your ⊞ cursor to the location for your button and click once.

11 Producing
Web Pages

Getting started in web mode

How easy is it to create your own website with PagePlus? It can be as simple as selecting a preset design template and editing the headings and accompanying text. And no matter how much customizing you choose to do after that, the whole job won't be nearly as complicated as developing your own site from first principles. So, if you're already comfortable using PagePlus for paper publications, you'll find it easy going. If you're just beginning, you'll learn to use PagePlus tools as you go.

Essentially, PagePlus takes the pages you've laid out and converts them to HTML.

Web design templates simplify things by providing you with a variety of starter layouts, professionally designed expressly for web display.

Starting a new web publication

Paper Publishing mode is the familiar PagePlus environment for creating print publications. However, before developing your website PagePlus must operate in **Web Publishing mode**. The Web Publishing mode includes special features, such as menu items and custom settings, to facilitate creation of web pages.

In this mode you'll then be able to create hotspots and animation effects, as well as add sound, video, and java applets. See PagePlus Help for more details.

To create a new web publication from scratch:

- Launch PagePlus or choose **New>New from Startup Wizard** from the **File** menu.

- In the Startup Wizard, select the **Start New Publication** option, select the **Web Page** category on the left, and choose your web page size (576x960, 720x1200, or 960x1536).

- Click **OK**. PagePlus will enter Web Publishing mode automatically.

To create a new web publication using a design template:

1. Launch PagePlus or choose **New>New from Startup Wizard** from the **File** menu.

2. In the Startup Wizard, select the **Use Design Template** option, select the **Web Publishing>Web Sites** category on the left, and examine the samples on the right. Click the sample that's closest to the site you want to create, then click **OK**.

3. Enter custom user details to personalize your website immediately.

If you'd like to build on previous work you've done with PagePlus, you can also take an existing paper publication and convert it to a web publication.

To turn an existing PagePlus (paper) publication into a website:

- Open the publication in Paper Publishing mode and choose **Switch to Web Publishing** from the **File** menu.

To adjust size/orientation of the current publication:

1. Choose **Page Setup...** from the **File** menu.

2. Set different page dimensions from the drop-down list or choose **Custom** for your own page size (enter page dimensions in pixels).

As with a paper publication, preparing a website for its unveiling means checking and rechecking the content. You can use the regular PagePlus checking functions such as Spell-checking, proofreading, using the thesaurus, etc.

In addition, the Layout Checker can inspect for (and often correct) text-specific problems, overlapping objects, or other conditions that will result in file sizes that are larger than necessary.

> Use standard Windows fonts or Websafe fonts for best results!

Choosing website colours

A website may have an adopted colour scheme, selected by using the **Schemes** tab. Each scheme has a name and consists of five complementary basic colours (plus additional web colours) which you can apply to any design element (see Using colour schemes on p. 227).

A selection of schemes (named "WWW 1" through "WWW 9") appearing at the bottom of the tab's scheme list are specifically designed for web use.

The currently set colour scheme is also shown at the bottom of the Swatches tab for convenience. For example for the colour scheme "WWW3", numbers or letters represent basic or web colour sets, respectively:

Web colours

Websites have several special **web colour** settings, usually defined as part of a colour scheme in the **Colour Scheme Designer**. You'll need to know about these settings, even if you haven't applied scheme colours to other elements in your site.

- The **Hyperlink** colour (labelled **H** above) applies to hyperlinked text **before** it's been clicked on.

- The **Followed Hyperlink** colour (labelled **F**), applies to hyperlinked text after a visitor has clicked to "follow" the link.

- The **Active Hyperlink** colour (labelled **A**), applies to hyperlinked text when a visitor's mouse button is depressed. Typically this is the colour shown after clicking and before the hyperlink's page is displayed.

- The **Rollover** colour (labelled **R**), applies to hyperlinked text when a visitor's mouse button rolls over it.

- A website's **Background** (labelled **B**) is a solid colour which will fill any blank space left in the browser when displayed on a larger screen.

- The **On-page** colour (labelled **O**) allows you to have a distinct colour for the defined page area. If set to transparent, it will display the current background colour.

Click the ·· button to access the Colour Scheme Designer (see p. 229).

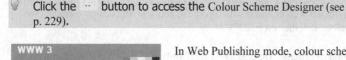

In Web Publishing mode, colour scheme samples in the Schemes tab show some web colours along with the five basic scheme colours, as shown at left.

The easiest way to apply new web colours is to select a different colour scheme by clicking a sample on the **Schemes** tab.

You can also change any of the web colours within a scheme using the Colour Scheme Designer, in the same way that you would modify the scheme's five basic colours. See Creating custom schemes on p. 229.

Using background images

You can include an image as a background instead of using the background colour at any time. Being part of a scheme, the image background will apply to all of your site's pages unless custom image backgrounds are used for individual pages.

To set a background image for a scheme:

1. Select **Colour Scheme Designer...** from the **Tools** menu.

2. Under Background Image Properties, click **Change**.

3. Check **Use Background Image**, click **Browse...**, and locate then select the image from the Import Picture dialog. Click **Open**.

- When checked, **Scrolls with page** scrolls the image background independently of the page contents in the browser window; if unchecked the background cannot scroll with page content.

- The **Repeat** drop-down list controls how your image is repeated on the background (Horizontal, Vertical, or Tiled). The option None places just a single image.

- The **Position** drop-down list sets the position of your image (e.g., Top Centre). For repeating image backgrounds, the image is repeated from this initial position. You can also specify a **Custom...** position, which sets the image's position in relation to its top-left corner.

4. Click **OK**.

All site pages using the scheme will possess the chosen image background.

Setting custom backgrounds

The web colours defined in the Colour Scheme Designer normally apply throughout the site, as described above, but you can use a background image or override the site's on-page and window background settings for any particular page instead.

To set a custom background image:

1. Select the page from the Pages tab.

2. Choose **Web Site Properties...** from the **File** menu.

3. From the dialog's **Background** tab, uncheck **Use Scheme Manager Settings** and check **Use Background Image**, click **Browse...**, and locate then select the image from the Import Picture dialog. Click **Open**.

4. Adjust the scrolling, repeating and position options.

5. Click **OK**.

To set a custom on-page and background colour:

- As above, but select a page colour from the **On-Page** drop-down list.

- For an off-page background colour, select a colour from the
  Background drop-down list. Select **More Colour...** to optionally pick
  from a Colour Selector dialog.

Choosing web page properties

There's more to creating a successful website than designing the pages. It's a
good idea to browse the **Site Properties** dialog, accessible from **File>Web Site
Properties** and review a variety of settings you might not otherwise have
considered!

Site Properties/Page tab

Some of the options on the dialog's **Page** tab pertain just to the current page,
while others apply to the site as a whole. The web page **title**, which will appear
in the title bar of the visitor's web browser, can serve to unify the pages and
focus the site's identity, as well as aid navigation. Each page in your site can
have its own title, but you may prefer to use the same title on multiple pages (in
effect, a site title). An easy way to do this is to start with a blank page, give it a
title, then replicate that page. Copies of that page will have the same title.

Each page also has a **file name** when it's published. You can specify file names
individually; otherwise PagePlus automatically generates them.

Check the instructions from your web service provider as to their naming
conventions for Home Pages and file extensions. By default, PagePlus names
your first (Home) page index.html—the standard file name a browser will be
looking for. Depending on the particular server in use, however, some other
name may be required. Likewise, the extension .htm is sometimes used for
pages.

Publishing a website to a local folder

Even though you may have saved your website as a PagePlus publication, it's
not truly a "website" until you've converted it to HTML and image files—in
other words, a format that can be viewed in a web browser. In PagePlus, this
conversion process is called publishing the site. You can publish the site either
to a local folder (on a hard disk) or to the web itself.

Publishing the site to a local folder lets you preview the pages in your own browser prior to publishing them on the web. You may find it convenient to keep your browser program open, and go back and forth between PagePlus and the browser. This way you can make changes to a single page in PagePlus, publish just the one page, then switch to your browser and preview that page to make sure everything appears just as you want it.

To publish the site to a local folder:

1. Choose **Web Site Properties...** from the **File** menu and double-check export settings, particularly those on the Graphics tab.

2. Choose **Publish Site>** from the **File** menu and select **to Disk Folder...** from the submenu.

3. In the dialog, locate the folder where you wish to store the output files by clicking the **Choose Folder...** button. You can create a new folder under any selected folder with the **Make New Folder** button. Click **OK**.

4. Either check the **Publish All Pages** option, or in the site structure tree, check which specific page(s) to publish. This can save a lot of time by skipping the export of pages you haven't changed.

5. Click **OK**.

After PagePlus has finished exporting the selected pages, you'll be asked if you want to launch your web browser to view your page. Click **Yes** to do this.

Previewing your website in a browser

Previewing your site in a web browser is an essential step before publishing it to the web. It's the only way you can see just how your PagePlus publication will appear to a visitor.

We'll assume you've already published your website to a local folder.

To preview your website from a local hard disk:

- Choose **Preview in Browser>** from the **File** menu, then choose a **Preview Page in <browser name>...** or **Preview Site in <browser name>...** to use an external browser.

The <browser name> will reflect which browsers are currently installed, e.g. the entry may read "Preview Page in Internet Explorer." If you have more than one browser installed, you can select which browser(s) to display on the submenu.

Publishing to the web

Publishing to the web involves a few more steps, but is basically as simple as publishing to a local folder! You can specify that all web pages are published or only pages updated since your last "publish."

To publish your site to the web:

1. On the **File** menu, choose **Web Site Properties...** and verify your export settings, particularly those on the **Graphics** tab.

2. On the **File** menu, choose **Publish Site>** and then select **to Web...**.

If this is your first time publishing to the web, the **Account Details** dialog opens (with no account information present). You'll need to set up at least one account before you can proceed.

3. In the **Account Details** dialog, enter FTP account details (obtained for your ISP) before clicking **OK**. See PagePlus Help.

   • If you've set up at least one account, the **Upload to Server** dialog opens. In the dialog, the last used account name is shown in the drop-down menu; its settings are displayed in subsequent boxes. You can use the drop-down menu to switch to another account, if you have set up more than one.

     You can also use the dialog to **Add** another account, and **Copy**, **Edit**, or **Delete** an account selected from the drop-down menu. It's a good idea to test your new or modified account by clicking the **Test** button—if the account details are valid, a dialog indicating successful connection displays.

4. Click the **Update Account** button. PagePlus seeks an Internet connection, then:

   • If uploading for the first time, selected files will be uploaded directly.
     - or -

- If uploading to an existing site (must be created with PagePlus), an **Uploading Files** dialog is displayed showing local file action (whether to **Add**, **Replace**, or **Leave** files).

  In the dialog, select either the **Incremental Update** or **Full upload** button. Choose the former to upload only files that have altered since the last upload. You'll see a message when all files have been successfully copied. Click **Close**.

Gathering server information

If you have an email account, your contract with the email service provider may allow you a certain amount of file space (e.g., 25MB) on their server where you can store files, including the files that comprise a website. Or you may have a separate "web space" arrangement with a specialized Internet service provider. It's up to you to establish an account you can use for web publishing.

Maintaining your website

Once you've published your site to the web, you'll need to maintain the pages on your site by updating content periodically: adding or changing text, pictures, and links, also file/folder deletion or renaming. Making the content changes is easy enough—all the originals are right there in your publication!

To maintain files and folders on your website:

1. Choose **Publish Site>** from the **File** menu and select **Maintain Web Site...** from the submenu. The Account Details dialog appears.

2. Select your FTP account name (from the drop-down menu), your Username and Password. Type the correct path in the Folder box, if required by your provider.

3. Click **Maintain**.

4. Use standard Windows Explorer conventions to perform maintenance tasks:

   - Click on the column headers to change the current sort, or drag to change the column width.

- The top row of buttons lets you view up one level, create a new folder, delete a selected item, upload/download a file, and refresh the window.

- Right-click to **Open**, **Download**, **Delete**, or **Rename** any file or folder.

- You can **Ctrl**-click to select multiple files or **Shift**-click to select a range of files.

- To move one or more selected files, drag them into the destination folder.

- To delete the entire web site, click the **View** button next to your selected Serif Manifest file—in the dialog, click the **Delete all managed files** button.

5. When you're done, click the window's ▨ **X** ▨ **Close** button to terminate the FTP connection and return to PagePlus.

12 Index